Computer Monographs

EDITOR: J.J. Florentin, Ph.D. Birkbeck College, London

Managing Software Projects

Managing Software Projects

J.K. Buckle M.A., F.B.C.S.

Macdonald and Jane's · London and
American Elsevier Inc. · New York

© J.K. Buckle 1977

Sole distributors for the United States and Dependencies and Canada:
American Elsevier Publishing Co. Inc., 52 Vanderbilt Avenue, New York,
N.Y. 10017

Sole distributors for all remaining areas:
Macdonald and Jane's, Macdonald & Co. (Publishers) Ltd.,
Paulton House, 8 Shepherdess Walk, London, N17LW

Macdonalds ISBN 0 354 04067 7
American Elsevier ISBN 0 444 19457 6
Library of Congress Catalog Card No. 76-53589

Text set in 10/12pt. Linotype V.I.P. Times, printed by and bound in Great Britain

To Jane, Karen and Jo
who will not understand a word of it.

Acknowledgements

The author would like to thank: Ted Humby for first suggesting that some notes made during railway journeys might form the basis of a book; Karen Sprague, Valerie Robson and my wife who between them turned almost illegible manuscript into typescript; and International Computers Limited for both providing me with the experience which underlies this book and encouraging me to publish.

Contents

1 Introduction

In recent years, the increase in the number of areas considered suitable for the application of a computer has been well publicised. To the computer professional, however, it is perhaps of more importance that the scope of individual applications has widened enormously. This has, in turn, led to an increase in the size and complexity of the total software needed to drive the system. The phenomenon is most easily seen in the software provided by computer manufacturers. These days, even with small to medium computer mainframes, a manufacturer is expected to provide complete operating systems comprising many thousands of instructions and involving investment of perhaps hundreds of man-years.

This type of complexity is not limited to manufacturers, and large-scale users of computers are making investments of a similar magnitude. Airline reservation systems are probably the most obvious examples but even in the less glamorous areas of 'routine' data processing the trend is away from individual invoicing, billing and payroll programs towards integrated processing systems. As more and more users come to regard their computers less as an engine to run programs and more as a part of a total information processing system, one can expect this trend to continue.

The need to produce software systems of this type in both the computer manufacturer and user areas has led to the development of new tools and techniques. There has been a movement from low-level to high-level implementation languages, design has become a more scientific process and less of an art, and entirely new operations have evolved such as the need to 'install' a total software system in an analogous fashion to the installation of machinery, rather than just test and issue programs. The complexity of the end product has also necessitated a new approach to managing the development, which can be loosely termed project management.

In a traditional data processing environment, where the work can be split into a number of independent programs which can be assigned to individual programmers or small groups of programmers, the manager's job is concerned mainly with ensuring that his staff progress satisfactorily towards well-defined targets and conform to well known standards and guidelines. In addition he is, of course, concerned with motivating, leading and the other personnel and administrative tasks which are common to any type of management. Such a job is as close to routine engineering production management as it is possible to get with the current state of the art of software.

A software project manager on the other hand needs to take complete responsibility for the over-all technical integrity of the system for which he is responsible. Throughout the life of the project he needs to control the continuous interactions between the various components of the system and the iterations between design, implementation and testing. He must allow for evolution of the product during the course of the project, while keeping a tight enough rein to ensure that the completed system meets the initial stated requirements within any specified constraints. And in addition he is still responsible for the allocation and use of resources and the budget- and man-management of conventional line managers.

The concept of a project manager is not, of course, new; project managers have been common in many branches of engineering for years. In some contexts, however, the term is used to mean a cross- or matrix-management appointment whose holder is responsible for 'ensuring' that a particular project is completed to schedule and specification, while the resources remain under the direct control of other line managers. Throughout this book, I assume that the project manager is in direct line charge of the software development project and has all the necessary resources under his control. This does not exclude, for example, the case where the computers used for the development of the system are run by other parties, providing the project manager has control of a sufficient budget to buy the service he requires. In this respect, his position is analogous to that of the manager of a large civil engineering project. He may decide, or be forced, to subcontract elements of the total development to third parties but the ultimate control and responsibility are his.

In the software development division of ICL we have, over the past few years, successfully moved from a traditional hierarchy of

2

line managers, with responsibility split on broad functional lines, to individual project managers for each major software product. The projects range from groups of related utilities up to a complete supervisor, and the team size, budget and experience of the project manager varies accordingly. Regardless of the size of the project, the goals of the project manager and the basic techniques used to achieve them are the same. This book is an attempt to set down in broad outline the duties of a software project manager and to give some indications of how these duties can be carried out. It is not intended to be comprehensive, so please do not be surprised if your favourite control or planning method is not mentioned. Rather, the aim is to draw attention to problem areas in project management and suggest possible solutions, leaving the details to the ingenuity of the individual manager.

I cannot claim that the book contains a single original thought; any merit it has arises from the fact that it brings together for the new project manager some well-tried concepts which would be regarded as second nature by experienced project managers. Indeed, so much of what follows is common sense that even a tyro project manager may consider it self-evident. Its justification for publication is that even experienced grandmothers can benefit from considering again the basic points of egg-sucking. All the information presented here is taken from other people's writings or from 'personal experience', a phrase which, to a great extent, means listening to or watching others. Wherever possible, I have tried to illustrate points by examples from projects. The projects themselves are imaginary but they bear an uncanny resemblance to actual projects I have known.

What follows, then, is intended as a checklist for managers responsible for the development of medium- to large-scale software systems. Although no deep technical knowledge of software is assumed, the advice is aimed at a technical manager. This is not because I believe that software projects could not be managed by non-technical, professional managers, but that I know of no examples of this and I intend to keep to well-trodden paths. The book does not constitute a mangement handbook in a professional management sense, and apart from some brief considerations in the final chapter, it is not concerned with motivating, leading and so on. These aspects are dealt with only where they are of particular interest to those whose job is the realisation of software products. Conversely, detailed technical software matters are discussed only where they have a direct impact on the management of the project.

It is easiest to describe the type of software project considered by examples. In terms of what is traditionally regarded as computer manufacturers' software, an obvious example is an operating system: a central supervisor plus the compilers and utilities necessary to provide a usable computer system for an applications programmer. However, the techniques discussed can be equally well applied to subsets of this, for example an individual compiler or any other than the most trivial utility. In the applications field the implementation of a large complex data base would certainly fall into the category of a software system requiring project management, but so too would a simple suite of programs based on a single set of files where intercommunication is important and detailed co-ordination and control are vital. In practice, I believe that any programming project which employs more than half a dozen people, or lasts more than six months, or breaks significantly new ground, requires the sort of control described in this book.

It cannot be emphasised too strongly that bringing a software system into existence is not analogous to the production of a car or even a computer mainframe. It is rather the equivalent of the initial design and prototype construction of the car or the computer, and the only equivalent of the production line in software terms is the replication of this prototype for use in several sites. For single user applications systems even this replication does not occur and the prototype we have constructed is, in fact, the end product. Indeed, the problems of software development are in practice much worse than the comparison with the development of a new model of car may suggest, and for this reason, although much of what follows could be taken to apply to any development activity, some is peculiar to software.

Because the software industry is still in its infancy, it is very rare for a development group to produce even similar things twice. New applications are often developed using new technology and new people. The design of a new car may sometimes reduce to a superficial restyling and the introduction of a well-tried engine from a larger model. Very rarely will all components be entirely new and even if they are, the chances of simultaneously introducing new technology are near zero. In software, on the other hand, we almost always start from scratch with each new project. As one speaker (Graham) said at the NATO conference on Software Engineering in 1968 'we build systems like the Wright Brothers built aeroplanes – build the whole thing, push it off the cliff, let it crash and start over again'. It is perhaps interesting that the car industry recognise the problems of major advances and that, for example, while Ford produced their conventional Mustang on time and within budget to a remarkable degree of accuracy, the development of an electric town car is considered to be a research project with an almost open-ended budget and timescale. The aim of software engineering is to get software from the electric car class into the Mustang class. This step is vital if costs are to be held to manageable levels and the NATO Conference reports (1, 2) should be essential reading for any software development manager. I shall refer to them again in what follows.

However, even if the software engineers succeed in establishing 'conventional' software, it will remain true that software systems are 'developed' not 'produced', and the methods and controls of a production line cannot be totally successfully applied. The following chapters are neatly compartmentalised into such areas as Planning, Design, Implementation, Organisation and Control. Readers should not be misled by the neatness. The divisions are, to a great extent, arbitrary and are intended primarily to split the subject matter into manageable sections. Development of a software system is a continuous process and the various areas interact in many ways; for example, some level of design must be accomplished before a total, meaningful plan can be drawn; organisation and control go hand in hand; and the methods chosen for control and implementation may seriously affect the plan. The project manager needs to consider all these areas simultaneously, all the time. The body of the book is intended to be read in its entirety before starting a project, and the final chapter contains a checklist for later reference during the development process.

To round off this introduction, can I apologise in advance for the use of unreferenced material. As I stated earlier, little of what follows is original, and where I remember it I have referenced my source material. Unfortunately, my memory for (hopefully) wise words is much better than my memory for names. Authors who find their ideas used without acknowledgement can at least have the consolation that their message got through to one reader, even if their name did not stick.

2 First steps

This section covers the initial steps that a project manager needs to take on receipt of his assignment. These are, of course, crucial to the success of the whole project since wrong decisions taken at this point may often be changed later in the project only at great cost.

Managers for software development projects may be appointed at any stage over an initial time window. This window starts when a problem is discovered and it is decided that a computer-based solution should be tried. If appointed at this stage the manager may be responsible for, or involved in carrying out, systems analysis, confirming or deciding that a new software development is required, carrying out cost analyses and so on. At the other end of the time window, the management appointment may be to implement a well-defined project using an existing project team. (We exclude here even later appointment to take over an ailing project in mid-development; the aim of the book is to avoid such happenings altogether!)

I feel strongly that the software development manager should be appointed as early as possible in the life of the project and should, if possible, be involved in the initial investigations into the necessity for and form of the new project. However, since the criteria for embarking on new projects (and indeed for using or not using a computer) are well outside the scope of this book, what follows assumes that at the time of the project manager's appointment it has been decided that:

● a new software development is needed.
● its objectives are known in outline.
● its potential users are known.
● some form of budget is available for it.

2.1 Get a 'customer'

From this starting point the project manager must determine the exact form of the development and then implement it. In order to do this it is essential that he establishes close contact with his potential users and maintains it, at both formal and informal levels throughout the life of the development. One sure way of developing a software disaster is to have a loose agreement from which both parties develop in different directions. This results in many costly changes during the implementation if the parties continue to talk to one another, or an unusable, unwanted system if they do not. The cost of such disasters can be orders of magnitude more than the more visible and well-known bogey of late software delivery.

It is dangerous for the project manager to assume he knows what the users really want or to rely on the opinion of a random sample of users in order to take implementation decisions. The first rule therefore is: find yourself a customer for the project. By a customer I mean a single person who can speak for all potential users about their needs, and carries their authority to decide on trade-offs when these needs conflict with each other or with implementation matters. Such a customer may be backed up by some committee of users' representatives if there are many of them. In such cases it is wise for the project manager to get involved with the committee to enable an exchange of raw information on needs and possibilities, but all formal negotiations should take place with a single person who has been approved by the other user parties. From here on I shall use the word 'customer' in this specialised sense.

In some cases, when real money is changing hands between the software developers and the commissioners of the software, a customer with the required specifications will almost certainly already exist. If not, it will be necessary to create one. If the development is an in-house one, the end users should be persuaded to appoint a representative; if the development is a speculative one intended for later sale either by itself or as part of a larger system, then the customer should be a marketing man who can represent the potential users at whom the product is to be aimed.

Having established a customer it is essential that the project manager treats him as a specialised member of the development

8

team ('us') rather than the other side of an interface with the users ('them'). Discussions should be as frank as possible and when decisions have to be made all alternatives should be presented, not just those favoured by the implementors. Such a well-informed and educated customer will always be able to get the users to accept unpalatable facts much better than any implementor could. The aim should always be to have you and your customer striving jointly towards a single goal rather than trying to wring as many concessions out of each other as possible.

.2 Establish feasibility

Having established a customer the next step for the project manager is to satisfy himself that the proposed software development is technically feasible in a broad sense and to establish a reasonable feel for the magnitude of the project. Details, costs and timescales will be open to negotiation later, but this will be the last time at which the project manager can say that he doubts the feasibility of the whole project without a considerable loss.

Discussion with the customer will establish the underlying needs of the users, and the requirements of the system can be compared with previous similar projects known to the project manager, or done earlier in the same establishment or by other companies. Many of the techniques described below under planning may be used to lesser depth at this stage.

If the project breaks new ground or involves large areas of uncertainty the project manager should insist on a feasibility study before proceeding further. Such a study should be of the shortest possible duration and be agreed with the customer. It must have clearly defined aims in the form of a list of questions to which answers will be provided and, arising from this, a well-defined end point.

One of the overriding questions that needs to be answered by such a study is: are the areas of uncertainty so great or so numerous as to constitute a research rather than a development project? If so, the overriding aims and objectives change and in general such projects lie outside the scope of this book. The project manager should never allow himself to be persuaded to accept a research project with the same objectives, constraints and resources as a development project.

It is extremely important both to have a distinct cut-off point between the end of any feasibility study and the start of the implementation proper, and to avoid the temptation to begin development before completion of the study 'to save time if the answer is yes'. In both cases the objectives of the study will be distorted to provide advance information for implementation purposes, it will be much more difficult to decommit even if this would be the most sensible course, and the project manager may find himself committed to implementation methods which he would not have chosen after further investigation. If a feasibility study is needed, then, ensure that its completion criteria allow a go/no go decision on the rest of the project and delay all other work on the project until this decision is made.

2.3 Make history

Even in the few hesitant steps taken so far we have seen the need to call upon historical details of previous projects. Unfortunately such details often exist as folklore or (only slightly better) in the memory of some individual participant. It should therefore be an important aspect of the project manager's job to document his development for use by future projects. Such documentation is by no means totally philanthropic since it is often essential to recall during maintenance and enhancement why certain decisions were taken, what assumptions were made and what alternatives were considered. Memory is too often clouded by later events so the advice to the project manager must be to establish a 'project log' at the earliest available opportunity.

The form of such a log is almost immaterial but in setting it up the manager must tread a careful line between not recording important details and recording so much unstructured information that the log becomes difficult or impossible to use. My own preference is for a top-level log which records only significant technical decisions, agreements with the customer, targets and actual results against targets and the like. This log can be backed up by meeting reports, technical papers, assessments, etc., to which reference can and

10

should be made in the main log. A counsel of perfection is to have in addition an index to current material by subject area. This requires considerable intelligent clerical effort especially in the early stages of the project, when ideas are being continuously put forward and rejected, but the effort pays off in later stages. This is particularly true if maintenance is likely to be in the hands of staff who were not involved in early discussions.

An area in which it is very important that good records are kept is that of predictions. The project manager should ensure that any time a prediction is made, be it about dates, resources, performance, or whatever, that this is recorded together with details of the conditions under which it was made, the point in the project at which it was made and any limits placed on its accuracy. He should also arrange that the actual value or date that is achieved in practice is recorded for comparison with the prediction. It is only by such careful recording that the accuracy of predictions can be improved. More will be said of historical records in later sections.

In conjunction with the setting up of the project log it is a good idea at this time to devote some attention to establishing a skeleton central filing system for the project. It has been said that there are two platonic filing systems: in one there is one file for each document, in the other there is one file marked 'miscellaneous'. Any real system is a compromise between these and it is advisable for the project manager to establish his own compromise before one is forced upon him. Individual project staff may well need their own copies of important documents but a central set which is always up to date is of great help as a reference base.

2.4 Define ends and means

The single most important thing that the project manager must do during the initial setting-up period is to establish a definition of the software system he is to produce in a language understandable by all relevant parties. The latter range from the future users to his implementing staff. This definition consists of two sets of restrictions on his future work which it is worthwhile to separate: the functional requirements for the finished product and the limitations placed on the methods open to him to achieve that specification. It is

11

necessary at the earliest possible stage to set down this information and to agree it with the customer as a common basis for future negotiations.

The definition should be as precise and detailed as possible. This is not to say that it will not change during the life of the project; it certainly will, but it should do so in a controlled way which allows all parties involved to see the consequences. Leaving flexibility in an initial definition merely delays and amplifies the eventual disaster. Remember that, since it is not possible actually to touch a piece of software development, it is difficult to convince either customer or junior implementor of the cost of late changes to specification and, without the discipline of an agreed definition under rigorous change control, costs in the most general sense are sure to escalate beyond the control of the project manager.

The first defining document then is what I shall call the Functional Requirements Specification (FRS). This is a definition of the facilities, performance, etc., that the users require in the finished product. All the basic information for this document comes from the customer and the document should be produced as a joint operation between the project manager and the customer. In producing this specification both parties should concentrate only on the final product and ignore intermediate releases, pilot schemes, dates and so on. There will be a strong tendency later in the project for these intermediate considerations to alter the form of the final product so it is well worth while at this stage to define an ultimate goal, unsullied by such matters, in the light of which later trade-off decisions can be made.

When drawing up the FRS the project manager should consider at least the following headings:

Facilities. This is a list of the functions the end user wishes the product to perform. They should be described in user-meaningful terms and are an essential tool to enable the project manager to keep his designers and coders on the right track. For this reason they should be defined with as much user-relevant detail as possible while leaving the implementation methods as free as possible.

Performance. Again this should be from the user point of view. Discuss with your customer from basic principles what it is he is really trying to do and discover what is important to him. Educate him if necessary on relative importance: for example '95% of all transactions done in less than 3 seconds each' is almost certainly a better criterion than 'average transaction time of 2 seconds'. Extend the performance area to cover size as well as speed – there may well be user limitations on in-store size and total size, independent of any implementation limitations.

Reliability. This is probably the most difficult area to quantify but it is of vital importance to the success of the product. Get from the customer as much information as possible on required up-time, mean time between breaks, break repair time and comparison with existing, similar systems.

Special requirements. Under this heading include such requirements as compatibility with existing systems, interface definitions, portability between different computer systems, adaptability and so on. Make sure the customer knows how much these things will cost and is prepared to pay for them, either in terms of performance reduction, or hard cash, or both.

It is almost certain that the first manifestation of the product will not meet this initial specification and it is as well to establish in advance the relative priority of the items in the FRS. The average user when asked to place ten items in order of priority will normally find nine items of priority one and one of priority two. It takes time to go back and persuade him to place his priority one items in the order 1A, 1B and so on, but this discussion is much easier at this stage in the project than in the emotion-laden circumstances of a predicted slip. Try to get the customer to distinguish first between his 'needs' and his 'wants' and refine from there. This information should also be placed in the FRS.

The FRS should be a much-used working document throughout the life of the project and it is important therefore to make sure that it is neither so large that it discourages frequent reference or so small as to be too vague. A dozen pages is a good target size but include references where necessary to other relevant documents: user descriptions, market surveys, competitive product descriptions, etc. (Alternatively, methods are available for producing non-textual 'models' of functional requirements. This approach leads more naturally into design. See for example reference 11.)

13

In parallel with the production of the FRS, the project manager should assemble a list of the constraints and non-functional requirements placed on his project in a Project Constraints Document (PCD). Some of these constraints may come from the customer but most will normally come from the project manager's own management. It is as important that these are written down and agreed as that the functional requirements are. Similarly, the constraints should be treated as candidates for trade-offs in the same way as the requirements. The main constraints are likely to be concerned with resources, releases and phasing.

The project manager should try to answer the following questions:

Resources. What financial budget is available for the project? What machine time is available? Are there limitations on the number of project staff?

Releases. What intermediate releases are required? Is a pilot project necessary? Are demonstrations needed before release? Who defines and monitors the criteria for release of intermediate and final versions?

Phasing. What are the timescales for final and intermediate releases if any? Which of these are vital and which desirable?

Other considerations. Are there any dependencies on other projects or from other projects which are imposed rather than being of the project manager's choosing? Are there any restrictions or house standards to be imposed on his methods of implementation, documentation, etc.?

The project manager should establish relative priorities for constraints as he did for requirements and include this information in the PCD. The PCD is likely to be a smaller document than the FRS since much more of the information is likely to be numeric and more references can probably be made to other documents. Aim for about half a dozen pages.

5 Control changes

The FRS and PCD together should form the basis for all further planning and for discussion with the customer and the project manager's own management. It is, however, important that these are living documents which reflect the current state of affairs as well as being historical records. On the other hand, it is necessary that changes are introduced in a controlled way, with the knowledge and agreement of all concerned. Since other documents may be produced with the same characteristics later in the life of the project, it is worthwhile for the project manager to set up a formal change control mechanism at an early stage.

Such a change control system should allow for the formal signing off of the FRS and PCD by the relevant parties: for the FRS these would normally be the project manager himself and his customer; for the PCD it would probably include the project manager's own management or whoever was responsible for allocating his budget. Following the sign off, changes should be made only by the signed agreement of the original signatories. Procedures should be established for circulating proposals for change (which can be put forward by any of the signatories), for commenting on them, for resolution of disagreement and for arbitration if necessary.

This formal system should, of course, be backed up by the earliest possible informal exchange of information between the parties concerned. If the project manager is given early warning of specification changes required by the user, or if the customer is kept in touch with project thinking it is much more likely that any change proposal raised will be quickly agreed. Indeed, the aim should be to have sufficient advance discussion to make sure that formal approval of a change is a rubber-stamping mechanism, but the formal mechanism is still required to ensure there is no misunderstanding and that all parties assume responsibility for the change.

Incidentally, when changes are approved do not throw away the old document or change proposal: they form useful historical evidence.

The general concept of change control will appear in various guises throughout the remainder of this book. In an area such as software development where visual indications of progress and

15

direction are almost completely absent, it is vitally important to have an agreed goal and an agreed path to it which are known throughout the project and among its potential users and patrons (the suppliers of budget and resources). There are two simple steps to achieving this:

(a) Commit the statement of agreement to paper and get all relevant parties to sign it off.

(b) Recognise that change is inevitable and set up a mechanism for introducing changes under control and with complete visibility.

The subject for agreement may be almost anything from plans or design descriptions to dependency definitions. The relevant parties may be different in each case but the change control concept remains the same.

2.6 Start planning

The final step in this first phase is to produce an outline plan. Such a plan should of course provide at the end a product which meets the FRS and conforms to the PCD. This may not always be possible and the project manager is then forced to renegotiate one or more of the restrictions placed on him: the budget, timescale, facilities, etc. Such negotiations should be carried out within the framework of the change control mechanism. The end of this activity should be an outline programme of work to which all parties are committed. The commitment should be spread as far as possible: if the project manager already has staff at this stage he should get them to commit to their section of the plan.

Availability of the draft plan completes the first step and launches the project proper. From this point on, the work that the project manager needs to do ceases to be a sequential set of jobs and becomes a set of interactive and sometimes iterative operations. For this reason, with one exception, the following sections are not time based but instead reflect areas of interest to the project manager which he may have to consider at various stages in his project. As an example the draft plan itself is merely the first output of a planning/replanning activity which will continue throughout the project. Details of the content and format of the pla are therefore dealt with under the general heading of 'planning'. The one exception is the

16

next chapter, which considers in more detail the timeslices into which the project naturally falls. The project manager's job does not change significantly from one slice to another, but his staff will be doing different things and this leads to changes in emphasis in the way in which the project manager carries out his work.

.7 Scenes from life

To illustrate this chapter let us consider an imaginary project. I have chosen a fairly small project so as not to confuse the major issues with too many details, but the points made are general ones. Consider a medium-sized computer installation with a central operations and software unit and a number of user departments. The installation supports a number of applications for individual departments as well as some relevant to all departments. From the latter a number of direct access files have been built up, more by accident than design, which form a central information base used by all departments. Most departments have terminals which are used for remote job and data entry purposes and there is a regular meeting of users to consider the service and possible future applications.

At one of these meetings it is decided to investigate the possibility of providing an inquiry system to interrogate, and maybe update the information base from the terminals. The software system supplied by the manufacturer provides some crude hooks for doing this but they are inconvenient and have to be supplemented in any case by purpose-built file search programs. The job of specifying the user requirements is given to a bright young user who promptly defines in great detail an interrogation language, its verbs, formats and default options. This language is easy to learn and use and provides the user with all the options he could possibly require. Unfortunately since no thought has been given to possible implementation methods, processing it could only be by *ad hoc* (and expensive) techniques. (Since this is not an anti-user book, let it be said immediately that had the job of definition been given instead to an implementor he would also have produced a detailed language definition. This would have been capable of implementation using a general algorithm of breathtakingly beautiful simplicity, but would

17

have been difficult to use and both input and output would have been incomprehensible to users without a Ph.D in Computer Science.)

Fortunately, at this stage a project manager designate is appointed from the central software unit, before the language definition can become a *cause célèbre*. He accepts the user's definition politely and attempts to extract from it the underlying requirements. He also prepares to convince the user departments that the user defined language is not ideal. Since he knows his implementation difficulties will not be a conclusive argument he does some coding estimates of certain important paths and from this deduces probable wait times compared with those that could be achieved if more attention were given to the implementation methods. He also prepares to show that copious default options, while making the user's task easier, gives the system less scope for consistency checks, which could result in a higher error rate. This will be particularly important if updating is to be allowed.

The project manager checks with the manager of the software unit in rough terms the amount of money and machine time and the number of men he can expect for his project and then persuades the user meeting to appoint a 'customer' to speak for them. During the period until the first draft plan is produced he spends a great deal of time with this customer and together they talk to other potential users. During the later design phase they will instead schedule a regular bi-weekly meeting to discuss progress and problems. These meetings will become less frequent during the coding and testing phases and will pick up again during integration and validation.

Since the project is fairly straightforward no feasibility study as such is needed but the project manager scans various journals for information on similar systems, talks to people he locates through user groups and societies about problems they have encountered, and discusses the system with the representative of the computer manufacturer. From the latter he learns that new, improved issues of the support software he will use are due later in the year, which may well affect his implementation strategy. To record these meetings and to keep the various information he is collecting he starts a single project file in which he places in simple chronological order all reports of meetings and relevant papers. This will form back-up material to the project log, the format and content of which he also

18

decides and writes down at this stage. The software unit maintains a central filing system and he decides to use this rather than start a new one of his own. He is assigned at this stage a fairly junior staff member and uses him to assist in the administrative work, but so as not to bore him completely, asks him to help locate relevant published material and, specifically, to consider how the product can best be tested.

Together with the customer, the project manager draws up a list of requirements which will form the basis of the FRS. The feasibility of the requirements is checked against the details of similar systems which are being accumulated.

The facilities required consist mainly of a list of the types of inquiries the system will support and the files on which they should work. These functions are grouped into 'essential', 'desirable' and 'possible' categories. The last category is worth including at this stage since some of its entries may be very cheap to provide and therefore worth doing. Performance is discussed and the types of inquiry grouped into priorities from this point of view. Target response time figures are assigned for these groups. It is apparent that the most important reliability consideration is that the central files should be protected from corruption as far as possible; this will have considerable effect on the implementation methods. However, targets are also set for other reliability standards. By considering the other jobs that this system will share the machine with, main store and backing store limits are also set. The proposed reissue of the manufacturer's software is discussed and it is decided not to rely on the improved facilities but to protect the interfaces with this software as far as possible so that the interrogation system can be moved to the new support software eventually. Further consideration of the performance aspects shows that changing the file structure could produce considerable savings in response time but at the cost of some upheaval, and the revalidation and possibly amendment of the existing programs which use the file. This trade-off is put to a full user meeting and it is agreed not to alter the files and to lower the performance targets accordingly.

Fig. 2.1 shows an extract from the project log during this period. The first entry records the decision reached on the version of manufacturer's software to be used. The statement is kept as simple as possible and a meeting report is referenced which gives reasons

19

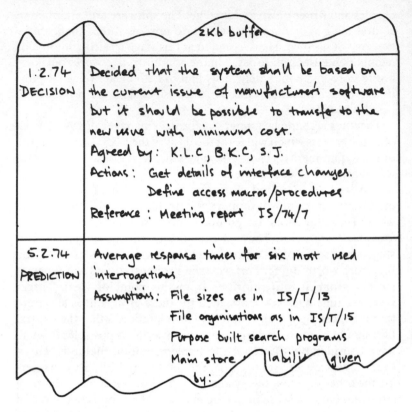

Fig. 2.1. Project Log Extracts

for the decision and other background information. The names of the people involved in the decision are noted as are some follow-up actions which are implied. The second entry is a record of a prediction of response times. Note that assumptions leading to the prediction are noted in considerable detail since they will be easily forgotten later while the actual figures will be remembered.

From discussions and predictions such as these an FRS is produced, agreed and placed under change control: two extracts from the FRS are shown in Fig. 2.2 and 2.3, and part of a change proposal for the FRS which is raised later in the implementation is shown in Fig. 2.4. In parallel with this operation the project manager has also

INTERROGATION SYSTEM   FRS/IS/1

Functional Requirements Specification

Contents

1.   Administration

          1.1   Change Control Records
          1.2   Document Cross References

2.   Summaries

          2.1   Need for the Product
          2.2   Potential Uses
          2.3   Outline of Facilities

3.   Facilities

          3.1   Functions
          3.2   Files Interrogated
          3.3   Options and defaults
          3.4   Capacities

4.   Performance Targets

5.   Reliability and Error Management Targets

6.   Special Requirements

          6.1   Use of Manufacturer's Software
          6.2   Standards
          6.3   Possible Enhancements

Fig. 2.2. Contents Page of a Functional Requirements Specification

6.   SPECIAL REQUIREMENT

6.1 Use of Manufacturer's Software

Initial implementation shall be based on issue 3.7 of the
Operating System as described in the System Manual, issue
7 and the release notice dated 7.11.73. However, in order
to facilitate transfer to issue 4 and later versions all
access to the procedures of section 8 of the manual will
be by means of macros under the control of the project
manager.

The utilities for upgra̶   ̶ dumping̶   ̶ designed
to ̶̶̶̶̶ or this por̶

Fig. 2.3. Extract from a Functional Requirements Specification

begun to build up a PCD. He goes into more detail of the staff that
will be available to him throughout the project, his budget limitations and the service he can expect from the computer. He ignores
demands from some users for the system to be ready the day after
tomorrow, establishes with his customer that a two stage release is
probably sensible and agrees target dates. He also notes the
documentation and other house standards to which the project will
conform, publishes the PCD and gets the relevant parts signed off
by the customer and his own manager. Fig. 2.5 shows an extract
from the PCD.

Finally, before beginning the project proper he draws up an
outline plan. In fact he has had draft versions of the plan around for
some time since he needed it to estimate resources and check the
feasibility of target dates. By the time he produces his plan, therefore, he is fairly sure that it is consistent with the FRS and PCD.
Examples of plans are given in Chapter 4. With the FRS, PCD and
outline plan approved the project officially starts.

INTERROGATION SYSTEM

F.UNCTIONAL REQUIREMENTS SPEC.

CHANGE PROPOSAL

CP 6
FRS/IS/3

PROPOSED BY: J.S.

BRIEF DESCRIPTION OF CHANGE PROPOSED

To replace the SEARCH function as currently defined by three separate functions.

REASON FOR PROPOSED CHANGE

The possible combinations allowed by the SEARCH function require a very general algorithm which cannot be implemented within the specified performance targets. Investigations with users show that the full power of the combinations will be rarely if ever used. The three new functions allow for efficient implementations of the common combinations and if used in sequence can provide the same facilities as the previous function but with less user convenience.

APPROVAL OBTAINED

Approved informally by reps. of all user depts.

DETAILED CHANGES

Remove section 3.1.4 of FRS/IS/3 and replace by the following.

Fig. 2.4. Change Proposal to Functional Requirements Specification

23

3. <u>RELEASES</u>

Two major releases are planned, ISR1 and ISR2.

ISR1 shall be to the full specification of the FRS as
far as performance, reliability and capacities are
concerned but relaxations are allowed in the functions,
files interrogated and options as detailed below. Target
release date for ISR1 to a single user for field trials
is:

<u>1.12.74</u>

with general release

<u>1.2.75</u>.

ISR1 sh~~~ ~~ntinue to b~ ~~~rted

Fig. 2.5. Extract from a Project Constraints Document

3 Project phases

After the first steps described in the previous section, the classical split for the project proper is into three sections: Design, Implementation and Testing, each of approximately equal duration. This is obviously an over-simplification since unit testing will take place during the implementation period and there will almost certainly be considerable overlaps between the phases. In addition maintenance and enhancement, which can easily account for half the total project costs, are ignored completely.

However, there is a way in which this conceptual split is of great importance to the project manager. The design stage is an analysis process in which a total system concept is broken down into components; in the implementation stage work proceeds on each of these components in parallel; and the testing phase is a synthesis process in which these components are brought together to form an actual system satisfying the original concept. The major problems in the synthesis and analysis phases will occur between the individuals involved in connected areas and the project manager's attention needs to be firmly focused on interactions, to ensure that the team are all moving in the same direction. During the implementation phase, on the other hand he has the (slightly) easier task of monitoring individual progress against plans and ensuring that there is no deviation from standards agreed in the design phase.

Diagramatically, the phases of a project can be represented as in Fig. 3.1. The resource curve applies equally to numbers of staff or total financial expenditure including machine time and supporting services. The peak in the testing period is common to all projects and the larger the project the more pronounced it becomes. Note also that although the resource needs fall off following this since, for a good project, the enhancement and maintenance period is likely to exceed the development period, maintenance costs are an important factor in the over-all system costs.

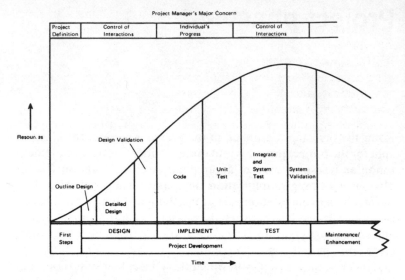

Fig. 3.1. Project Resource Graph

The following sections deal with the project manager's role during the various stages and with related decisions he must take.

3.1 Design

Throughout the initial steps of the project, it has been possible for the manager to remain in total control of what was going on, even if he used some assistance. Entering the design phase, for any but the smallest projects, it becomes necessary to delegate major areas to other people. For this reason it is essential that all staff engaged in the design phase are working on the same product!

A sensible way of beginning the design stage is to hold some form of seminar for all design staff at which the project as defined in the FRS and PCD is discussed in the presence of the customer and any other potential users that he may care to bring. Such a meeting should not only cause the design staff to begin thinking along the same lines but should establish a close relationship with the customer which can continue throughout the design phase. The design

26

team should regard the customer as a resource available to them to provide information on user needs and assessment of possible ways of progress.

The choice of design methods and tools is largely a technical matter and therefore outside the scope of this book. Whether design is top-down (starting at the system level and progressively decomposing down to module level), or bottom-up (starting with module design and synthesizing a total design), or starts at some intermediate point and works outwards, will be largely determined by the nature of the problem and the previous experience of the design team. However, it is worth bearing in mind that, all other things being equal, a top-down approach tends to be more easily audited and controlled by the project manager. Of even more importance from his point of view is that a unified approach should be adopted throughout the team. Therefore whatever method is chosen and for whatever reasons, the project manager must establish that as a standard for use throughout the project.

There are a number of other important standards that are needed. For example, it is necessary to record the design in a standard way: is the project to use a formal design language, or a diagrammatic or computer based recording system, or will it rely on narrative descriptions and flow charts? Whoever decides, it is the project manager who must enforce the standard. Again, there is no common agreement on the level of detail at which design ends and coding begins. Here some flexibility is possible and it may be convenient to go for greater detail in some areas than others, but it is important to define at an early stage the criteria for completion of the design to avoid both starting coding before the design is complete, and the less common fault of holding up coding for unnecessary design detail.

Modularity within design and construction is synonymous with righteousness in technical circles these days, and the project manager should remember that modularity can also provide a good management tool to enable realistic measurement, and permit a division of labour in later stages. Control becomes easier if all modules are approximately the same size, even though this may not completely accord with a logical division of functions. It is therefore wise for the project manager to specify his requirements as standards at the outset. He should also not allow the designers, in

27

splitting up the product into modules, to be over-influenced by the ability and areas of expertise of the staff who will be producing them. Such forethought is useful providing it does not tie the project manager's hands in organising his team as he thinks best in later stages, and providing it does not imply that the loss of one member of the team can jeopardise the project.

Once a design has been produced, at any level of detail, it is essential to record it and place it under change control for the next stage. Regardless of the design approach, a hierarchy of documentation is useful in this respect, with the top level design in one document, the next level down split into several documents which are expansions of the main sections of the top level and so on. During the early design stages changes will be frequent and it is therefore important that they can be agreed and the documentation updated quickly, if the latest working design is not to be found on the backs of envelopes. For this reason the authorities for approving changes should be different at each level. At the top level the project manager will probably wish to be involved and maybe even the customer. At lower levels, providing changes do not percolate upwards, only those parties immediately concerned within the design team should be required to approve. Incidentally it is wise to regard the FRS and the PCD as integral parts of the design documentation and it may be worthwhile at this stage to expand the FRS into a full functional specification, showing how the requirements will be met. This will be discussed again in the section on documentation.

The hierarchical design description will normally be in terms of procedural modules. Of equal importance are interface definitions, data structure definitions and table formats used by the procedures. While it is sensible to remove many data definitions from the majority of procedural modules by access macros or procedures, in order to preserve flexibility, it is still necessary to record them and subject them to change control.

Although the computer industry spends a great deal of effort encouraging users to implement ever more ambitious applications, and although computer-aided design is a well-founded discipline, surprisingly little use is made of computers in designing software systems. If he has suitable access to a computer during the design stage, the project manager should seriously consider its use for recording the design in formal terms, checking the validity of changes or new sections of design, and possibly simulation for performance prediction purposes. Simple use for these purposes may involve only standard available software, while for large systems it may be worthwhile to create a total new system for the purpose (see, for example, reference 5).

If the project manager does decide to use the computer for design control purposes, in addition to the warnings set out under 'Implementation Tools' below, there are two other considerations he should bear in mind:

> First, make sure that the computer is used only for the things it is good at; the division between what is to be done by the human designers and what is to be done by the system should be carefully chosen.
>
> Second, ensure that the requirements of the project are properly 'sized', and that the system performance and available machine time will meet this need.

To do the second of these it is necessary to estimate the number of design changes, simulation runs or whatever, that will be needed throughout the project and to calculate the turnrounds achievable at the peak rates of usage. This is essential, for if the turnround means that at some point in the project it will become a holding factor, giving rise to supplementary manual systems, the computerised system will almost certainly be more of a hindrance than help.

When the design is thought to be complete it is necessary to validate it before proceeding to coding. Design errors which get through to the coding stage are often the most expensive type of error to cure. Various methods can be used for the validation including independent audits, trial coding of important sections, or top-level procedures, and computer simulation. One checking technique of use both at this and earlier stages is the 'walk-through'. This involves the design team, or some subset of it, getting together to trace a particular important path through the design with each member acting out the operations of the modules for which he is responsible. Walk-throughs usually clarify the relationship between separate design areas very well and in addition often pinpoint unnecessary paths and 'holes' in the design.

29

To end this section I have two pieces of advice for the project manager. The first is to accept in the design only those things which are easy to explain. This applies whatever the descriptive medium. If the description is lengthy and inelegant there is a high probability that it has not been thought out properly, or that it does not cover all the cases, or that it is ambiguous, or that it is inefficient, or all of these. Secondly, constantly monitor the relative complexity of the various areas of design. If any area shows signs of being much more complex than the rest this is often the result of a bad design decision one level up.

3.2 Implementation tools

Before the project passes into the coding stage the project manager must decide in what language the coding is to be done. Indeed, he may be wise to make this decision early in the design stage since the implementation language may well influence or constrain the design. Much has been written elsewhere of the battle between high- and low-level languages and I do not intend to go into detail here (see for example section 4.3.4 of reference 1). Suffice it to say that if the high-level language chosen is consistent with the design (or vice versa) and a good compiler and associated system exists, the cost of implementation is considerably reduced and maintenance and enhancement are also easier and cheaper. The counter argument is of course efficiency. It is certainly true that for small programs or modules a good low-level coder can normally produce smaller faster code than a good high-level coder, even with a good compiler, and there are some areas of system which may be sufficiently time- or size-critical to demand low level coding for this reason.

My personal view is that the advantages of a high-level language are such that the default choice should be a suitable high-level language with low-level languages used only where it can be proved that the efficiency they give in space and/or time is essential to meeting the product requirements described in the FRS and PCD. Even in the latter case it may be possible to restrict low level use to specific areas of the product and it is by no means necessary to descend all the way to assemblers to achieve control over the coding. Languages such as BCPL (3), CPL1 (10) or PL/360 (4) can provide the sort of efficiency and control of the machine required without sacrificing all the desirable features of high-level languages. If an assembler cannot be avoided at least consider using it in conjunction with a macro-processor; with sufficient control of the macro definitions this can give many of the advantages of a high-level language.

The choice of an implementation language will, of course, depend not only on the suitability of the language itself for the job in hand but also on the availability of a suitable compiling system. This means not only a compiler but an operating system with editing and filing utilities, and these are only a part of the total tools that any medium-to-large-scale software development will require. Some form of simulator may be required during the design process to validate algorithms or assumptions, and a test harness to assist in unit testing will certainly be needed. The cost of production of such tools may amount to a considerable proportion of the total budget and the project manager should never underestimate it. There is always a tendency among programmers to extend a great deal of energy on tools because they are often far more interesting than the main project and less constrained. This tendency needs to be carefully controlled.

The manager should try to use existing tools wherever possible, if necessary modifying them to suit his needs. Development of new software is difficult enough at the best of times without basing it on new tools and technologies as well. Both the cost and the risk of failure should be weighed against any benefit that might be achieved. If in spite of this the manager feels there is no alternative to producing his own tools, he must subject the production to the same degree of control as the main project. Insist on detailed objectives and constraints; appoint a sub-project manager and get him a 'customer' within the main project; and make him plan to the same standards as the project proper. Incidentally if new tools have to be produced never allow them to be made outside the project. Having a separate development on which the project is vitally dependent which is not under the project manager's control is a recipe for disaster.

The strictures against new tools do not apply if the tool is a component of, or a step towards, the final product itself. Plans, for

31

instance, to bootstrap a compiler written in the language it is going to compile or to write and use archiving and editing utilities which will form part of the final product are to be applauded. They provide the product with early, critical use and establish its good and bad points before the real user has to suffer.

Whether implementation tools are old or new it is essential that each of the implementors is completely familiar with them by the time they are used in anger. The project manager should include familiarization as part of his plan as well as allowing for a running-in period for any new tools.

3.3 Coding

Although it may be desirable to start coding in certain areas before completion of all detailed design it is important that individual members of the project team do not drift into coding without management control. There is a great temptation having completed a section of design to start coding it immediately. Unfortunately decisions in other design areas may invalidate such early coding, leading either to rewrites or, worse still, mismatches which are not discovered until integration begins. The project manager's aim should be to discard as little code as possible. This implies delaying coding until there is a high chance that what is to be coded is what will be required in the final product.

It is worthwhile making the official start of coding a recognisable occasion to the project team. The project manager should start this phase by holding meetings with all project staff to ensure that they are familiar with the over-all design and the total implementation plan, as well as with the individual parts with which they will be concerned in the coding phase. It is also worthwhile in these meetings to go over again the objectives and constraints of the project in case they have been temporarily lost from sight during the interactions of the design phase. Individual project staff may be helped by discussion with the customer to see how he views the area with which they are concerned. This helps to counter the all too familiar implementors' complaint that 'it wasn't meant to be used like that'!

Whatever language has been chosen for implementation, it is essential that the project manager controls how it is used in the coding phase. This control is needed both to avoid any on-the-fly redesign by the coders and to allow him sensibly to measure progress. Control should be imposed by stating standards, conventions and advised tactics, not only for coding but for use of tools in general. Remember, though, that standards must be capable of being imposed or they either fall into disrepute or are bypassed in secret, leaving the project manager with a false sense of security. Standards which are self-policing are the best: if possible always alter the compiler to make a construct illegal or flagged rather than just banning its use. If self-policing is not possible keep the standard simple and capable of easy audit.

Coding is normally associated with 'unit test', that is the check out of the individual modules coded, and both operations are usually carried out by the programmer. From the project manager's point of view, however, unit testing must form part of a total testing and validation strategy and is dealt with in a later section.

Finally, it is very easy to overemphasise the importance of the coding phase. This is probably because in the early days of computers the coding of small machine code routines was a large percentage of the job of getting them to work. Today with large software systems to be produced and more sophisticated implementation tools this is no longer true. Although programmers dislike being called coders there is still a folk memory in the industry which tries to equate the two operations. Another look at Fig. 3.1 will show that coding only occupies approximately one-sixth of the total time of the implementation period (and about the same proportion of the resource usage) compared with one-third for design and about one-half for integration and testing. In addition, monitoring during the coding phase is easier for the project manager than at any other time for the reasons set out at the beginning of this section. Thus, although from a technical view point it is important to get the coding right, from a project management point of view the focus should be elsewhere.

4 Integration and tuning

Once several units of the system have been coded and tested by themselves the more complex task of integration can begin. Before this point, the project manager should have decided upon, and

33

promulgated, the strategy to be employed. One important aspect of this is the organisation of the team. At one extreme one can have the integration carried out by the coding team themselves; at the other extreme it can be done by a separate body of people with formal handover procedures. The first of these has many advantages from the technical point of view and means that knowledge of the modules is directly available throughout the integration operation. It has the disadvantage that control, and more particularly, monitoring by the project manager becomes more difficult since the boundary between coding and integration can be blurred. In addition there is great scope for confusion between various tested and untested versions of modules.

On the other hand establishing a separate team provides a very good basis for monitoring since one can easily measure at any time the number of modules accepted by the integration team, the number of corrections made, the number returned and so on. Disadvantages are that, since the integration team will in general be unfamiliar with the individual modules there will be a considerable training period before they can obtain the required level of knowledge. This will be exacerbated by the fact that with this sort of organisation the coders will often have moved on to other modules or other projects when they are most needed.

A compromise which the author can recommend is to have the coding staff perform the integration of their own modules but to an integration plan produced outside the coding team and using a small service team responsible for maintaining the libraries of integrated and unintegrated modules, test programs, etc. The service teams can also set up the integration and testing computer runs if desired and can certainly maintain statistics.

Whatever organisation is chosen it is absolutely essential that the project manager is personally in day-to-day control of the integration phase. To say that a module is half coded is a bad enough measure of progress but at least the number of lines coded can be compared with an estimate of final size. To say that a system (or module) is half integrated is meaningless. It is vital for the project manager to have a step-by-step integration plan with well-defined milestones against which progress can be measured; more of this later.

Change control is of great importance during integration but unlike earlier sections we are here talking mainly of controlling changes to code rather than definitions. Each new version of a module produced should have a version number and be accompanied by a statement of what changes have been made and for what reason. It is worthwhile setting up a formal reissue system for this purpose which can form a pilot scheme for the system that will be used to issue amendments when the software system is in productive use. If 'fixes' are to be made to integrated modules temporarily to correct or bypass errors, ensure that these are done openly, are well documented and are replaced by a new issue of the module as soon as possible.

The project manager should ensure that the integration staff maintain a set of regression tests which check out aspects of the whole system whenever a new or revised module is integrated. To minimise the confusion that will inevitably exist during this period, it is wise to maintain a register of all modules showing:

- whether they have been integrated, or are about to be integrated or are being unit tested, etc.
- the current version number.
- where the module can be found (i.e. in which library, where a backup copy is, etc.).
- who is responsible for the module.

It is essential that this register is kept up to date. It may be sensible to use a computer to maintain the register. If so ensure that a fast turn round is possible both for updating and printing or displaying the register.

In a similar way to the issue system, a pilot error reporting system should be set up as soon as possible. It should provide means for logging known or suspected errors, assigning them a reference and recording who is responsible for pursuing each one. It is also often convenient to assign priorities to errors and establish in detail the procedures to be followed for each type. Statistics kept during this period will be invaluable in improving the maintenance service after issue and for estimating the level of resources that will be required. As with the issue system it may well be sensible to use a computer to help, but make sure the turnround requirements can be met by a careful sizing exercise.

Besides controlling changes to modules and/or the system, the

35

project manager must ensure that these changes during integration are reflected in the documentation, all the way back to the design documentation if necessary. This is a very difficult task since the programmers normally find it boring, while documentation specialists find it difficult to get information or detect the ramifications of changes. One possible method is to make the programmers responsible for the up-to-dateness of their documentation but to have a full-time documentation chaser who asks pertinent questions, and bullies and threatens in order to ensure that it is not forgotten.

Once the system is integrated it is often followed by a tuning stage when inefficiencies in the operation are discovered and removed. This may begin immediately or, if the initial try at producing a system gives a reasonably satisfactory performance, it can be delayed until after a first issue and treated as part of the enhancement programme. There is one golden rule for tuning: don't start doing any before you have a working system. By all means measure the performance from the earliest possible opportunity but attempting to remove performance problems before a total system exists will rarely be cost effective and can be dangerous. Once the system works as an entity it will be possible to isolate the critical performance areas and work on them in the context of the total system operation.

It is worthwhile also remembering that, especially if a high-level implementation language has been used, considerable performance improvement can often be obtained by concentration on the production tools. The Multics system was coded mainly in a PL/I subset called EPL. To quote David (1), 'Major improvements were made by improving the EPL compiler (3 times), by capitalising on experienced programmers' ability to produce EPL code which compiled for fast execution (3-10 times) and by changing strategies in the system to optimise its performance (3-10 times).' He goes on to quote particular modules which were reduced by factors of between 4 and 26 in size and improved by factors of between 8 and 60 in performance for a cost of 3 man-months per module or less.

To be able to carry out such improvements it is of course necessary to be able to monitor performance easily. This is something which the project manager should ensure is considered and planned for throughout the design and coding stages.

.5 Testing and validation

Dijkstra (2) has said that program testing can be used to show the presence of bugs, but never to show their absence. This cannot be denied. Every possible attempt must be made both to reduce the generation of errors and to *prove* that no errors exist. However since there is as yet no agreed technology for doing this, in the general case some testing will be required. It is important that the project manager establishes early in the project an over-all testing strategy against which testing plans can be prepared.

It is psychologically important that the business of testing is looked at in the right way by all team members. Testing, using valuable machine time, must never be regarded as a substitute for good design and careful coding. The aim of a module coder should always be that a test run finds no errors. Conversely the aim of a designer of a test run should be that every test should be cost effective and therefore throw up as many errors as possible. The testing strategy should specify standards for such things as desk checking to be carried out on modules, the way in which unit testing is to be done and methods of testing integrated subsystems as well as the whole system. Formulation of the strategy will involve the definition of testing tools as well as test programs: for example, a specialised test harness for supplying parameters to, and reading results from individual modules may be required. The use of such tools should be made obligatory and plans for their implementation need to be drawn up. Standards for the implementation should be as formal and as rigorous as for the main project. Similarly plans are needed for obtaining or implementing the necessary test programs and if at all possible checking them out independently, to ensure that they do not themselves contain errors which will later be attributed to the system under development.

In the heading of this section I have used the terms 'testing' and 'validation'. Both activities should be included in the testing strategy and the overall test plan. The difference is mainly one of emphasis: the main aim of testing should be to find and remove as many bugs as possible from components and finally from the whole system. Validation should be an attempt to prove to both the project manager's and the customer's satisfaction that the product

37

will meet its specified requirements. Although many of the same techniques are used in each of these stages I believe it is worthwhile to separate the two and probably to employ a different organisation of the team in the two phases.

During the testing, or debugging phase, both for unit testing and testing during integration, the best results are usually obtained by making the coding or integration teams responsible for the production and running of their tests. In general during these phases the best knowledge of what is likely to go wrong (and therefore requires testing) exists in these teams. The only danger is that given the individual team members' preoccupation with their own areas and the natural optimism which exists among programmers, some apparently simple aspects may not be checked out and some interactions between areas may be overlooked. A way of handling this is to have a separate person responsible for vetting and approving the individual plans in the light of these probable deficiencies. He should also audit the actual running of the tests and make sure that no tests are dropped or altered without his permission. This sort of organisation, where the producers have testing responsibility and are merely audited is almost always better than a separate testing team who specify and run the tests. The latter organisation is liable to divert the producers' undoubted ingenuity into devising ways of passing the tests with the greatest ease without regard to the actual efficiency in discovering errors.

Validation on the other hand is not supposed to begin until the production phase is thought to be complete. Ideally it should merely be a rubber-stamping process to prove that the product is viable. For this reason it is better separated from the main programming team and it should certainly employ in the main test material that has not been used during the testing phase. Validation should also cover wider aspects than testing normally does. For example, the user and operational documentation should be validated against the actual system. Again although testing should concern itself with error paths, the validation operation should take particular care to try to use the system badly, as well as to check its resistance to corruption.

It is important that the final system testing, and in particular the validation, approximates as closely as possible to the actual use that the end users will make of the system. The customer should be closely involved with the definition of the validation tests and should be asked if possible to provide material and perhaps assistance.

Validation should also ensure that the system works throughout the ranges of hardware and supporting software variations contained in the FRS. With large, complex software systems it may be worthwhile to follow the validation phase by a field test, that is a live use in some restricted circumstances. This allows the general problems of introduction of a new system to be encountered and overcome in the context of a limited number of users who can be persuaded to regard themselves primarily as an aid to the implementation team rather than as paying customers.

Validation (or field testing if it is employed) must be followed by a handover of the product to the end users. It is wise to do this formally by means of an acceptance test agreed between the project manager and the end users which signals that the product has reached an agreed state of development. The acceptance test may be an entirely new test, defined by the project and end users together, or it may consist of the customer monitoring certain milestones in the validation tests. The important thing is that both parties should agree that passing the test ensures with some degree of certainty that the system is usable. This should in turn mean that the users will feel obligated to try to use the system effectively rather than throw up their hands and call in the implementors at the first sign of trouble.

One of the problems with testing is that software systems can be 'taught' to pass particular tests. By this I mean that a faulty run can cause corrections to be made which allow a correct run without removing a general problem. During the testing phase this is not especially troublesome. Unfortunately a count of the number of successful tests is not a good measure of the product quality under these circumstances since there is no evidence that the product can pass any new test without alteration. A much better measure is the number of *new* tests that can be run without error. A compiler provides a good example: having successfully compiled a number of test programs which demonstrate that the major features of the language can be dealt with, the best measure of the state of the compiler will be the percentage of new programs (or lines of source) which can be compiled without error. It is therefore wise for the

39

project manager to assemble more test material than he expects to use in order to provide new tests if needed. This is particularly true during validation. If too many faults occur it is no use putting them right and carrying on. The correct course should be to cancel the validation attempt, correct the bugs found and any others that can be discovered, and then restart validation from the beginning using new material.

The foregoing has been mainly concerned with proving the presence of facilities. Two other areas need to be tested and validated as being to specification: the performance and reliability. Functional testing is by comparison easy since tests can be devised to specifically test the availability of specified functions. Performance which can cover, apart from the obvious question of speed, such matters as store occupancy, operating efficiency, file usage and so on, is best done by measurement of the required parameters during the functional testing. This requires careful planning and the statement of testing strategy must include details of what needs to be measured and at what stages. This will in turn lead to requirements for measuring tools – hardware or software monitors – and obtaining or implementing these must appear as part of the development/testing plan. The project manager should make sure that 'measurability' is built into the product.

Testing reliability is even more difficult. The only way of proceeding here is to work back from the final reliability requirements as specified in the FRS. These should be in terms of the expected error rate, mean time between breaks, uptime, repair time, etc., for the final system. It will then be necessary to work back in time estimating the expected values of these or associated parameters at various stages in the project and to establish this as part of the development plan. 'Testing' the performance then consists of recording the actual values of these parameters during the functional testing, for comparison against the plan. It may also necessitate particular runs being scheduled specifically for performance testing purposes. For example, early functional tests of a system will normally be short and to obtain information on reliability it may be necessary to devise runs which exercise the system for greater periods of time.

The project manager must always bear in mind that, whatever the customer may say when defining his needs, performance and reliability are normally of greater importance to him than facilities. This is because a user can often take his own steps to avoid the effects of a missing facility, but there is little he can do about the other two areas. The testing strategy must therefore pay at least equal attention to all three aspects to ensure that there are no nasty surprises at the last moment, when all the facilities are present but the product is still unusable.

.6 Maintenance and enhancements

Enhancements to an issued software product can be of two types. If at the beginning of a project it is decided to have a first general issue which does not meet all the known requirements, the later issues which introduce the required level of performance or facilities may be regarded as an enhancement program. The requirements should be documented as such in the FRS and should have a draft plan made for them at an early point in the project. This plan will need to be fleshed out around the time of the first issue.

When the need for this type of enhancement is known from the beginning of a project it is valuable to include the full requirements in at least the initial design phase, and then freeze those sections of the design documentation. This will help to ensure that decisions are not taken during the detailed design or coding stages which make the enhancements difficult or impossible. However open-ended a designer tries to be, his chances of success are small unless he has a fairly clear idea of the direction in which his product is to be extended.

The other type of enhancements are those which arise during the life of the project or after its first issue. These may be caused by the project team, or the customer, or the actual users, realising that certain improvements are desirable (or essential) or they may result from agreements between the user and project team to delay certain requirements from the first issue in order to meet timescale, resource or budget constraints.

Enhancements generated during the life of the project will often be of a general nature: 'improve the performance', 'make the operator's job easier'. As soon as possible these should be made specific by monitoring the area which requires improvement and deciding the detailed changes which need to be made. This detail

41

should then constitute the FRS for the enhancement programme since the vaguer initial statements are too open to implementations at a tangent to the real requirements.

Enhancements of both kinds should be fully documented as they arise and added to the FRS. Towards the end of the main development activity the project manager will need to negotiate with his customer the form of the enhanced product and draw up a new development plan. From this point on the process is identical to the initial development and the steps are the same.

Maintenance is another matter altogether and is needed whether or not there is an enhancement program. Resources will certainly be required to support and hold the hands of users, to investigate suspected faults, to document and correct errors and so on.

This effort should be planned for from the beginning of the project, to ensure that key staff are not earmarked for work on other projects as soon as the first issue is made, or at least to ensure that suitable replacements are trained in time. This is particularly important where there is a scheduled enhancement program since there will be a great tendency for important team members to work full time on the enhancements even before the first version is issued, in the belief that they will be available to answer queries on the first version when required. This never happens. The enhancement and maintenance programs must be planned and resourced independently even though they will undoubtedly interact with each other and although there is sometimes a very fine distinction between enhancements and error corrections!

The effort required for maintenance will depend directly on the error correction rate for the product. This in turn depends on three factors:

- the bug rate for the product, i.e. how many bugs are found in the product over a given period of time.
- the difficulty of isolating and correcting bugs once found.
- the number of different users: different users always find different bugs.

At the beginning of the project the third factor should be known and estimates can be made for the other two, based on knowledge of similar projects. As the project goes on these initial estimates can be updated using the experience gained during testing, integration and validation. For this reason it is advisable to institute a recording mechanism for these statistics as well as identifying specific replanning points at which the maintenance effort required can be re-estimated.

The other important aspect of maintenance is documentation. At some stage during maintenance it is almost certain that all the original project development staff will move on and the documentation must be good enough to allow the remaining team to carry on. Maintenance and support staff will certainly require the design and implementation documentation and may also need specialised maintenance information. More of this in a later section.

.7 Examples

Let us follow the fortunes of the interrogation system described in Chapter 2 a little further, to put some flesh on the bones of this chapter.

Following a seminar of all his project staff, his customer and other user representatives, the project manager and his senior staff produce an outline design document of half-a-dozen pages as a guide to the design strategy to be adopted and the standards to be employed. They decide on basically a top-down design and a narrative approach to the design documentation supported by flow-charts, diagrams and tables where necessary. The design strategy document forms 'level 0' of the documentation hierarchy and the design team go on to produce the level 1 document. This runs to about 60 pages, of which half are flow charts, table layout diagrams and file formats. The contents list of this document is Fig. 3.2.

The document begins with an outline specification and a description of the environment in which the system works. This refers back to the FRS. Subsequent sections describe the interfaces with system software, file descriptions, data definitions, formats of interrogation commands and replies, and module descriptions. This last section begins with a module map (see Fig. 3.3) and goes on to describe the individual modules in terms of their functions, interfaces, cross-references to data and the outline flow chart. The module section is further expanded to provide level 2 documentation with individual coding specifications for modules and service routines and more

43

INTERROGATION SYSTEM   DS1/IS/3

Design Specification - Level 1

Contents

1.   Administration

      1.1   Change Control Records
      1.2   Document Cross References

2.   Outline Specifications

3.   Working Environment

      3.1   Machine Configuration
      3.2   System Software

4.   Software Interfaces

      4.1   System Interfaces
      4.2   Communications Interfaces
      4.3   File Management Interfaces

5.   File Descriptions

      5.1   Parent Files
      5.2   Overflow Files
      5.3   Work Files
      5.4   Test Files

6.   Data Definitions

      6.1   General Conventions
      6.2   Dictionary of Common Areas

7.   Message Formats

      7.1   Prompts
      7.2   Responses
      7.3   Error Messages

8.   Module Descriptions

9.   Service Routines

Fig. 3.2. Contents Page of a Level 1 Design Document

44

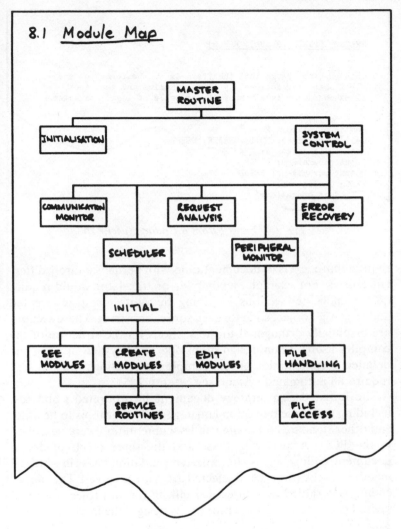

8.1 Module Map

Fig. 3.3. A Module Map

detailed flow charts and diagrams where necessary. Part of a sample coding specification is shown in Fig. 3.4.

(This documentation is comparatively compact because the project is essentially a simple one. More complex projects would

```
SRECRF  (FIELD, RESULT, ERROR)

This routine checks that the field is in the format of one
alpha character followed by seven numerics and that the
alpha character is a member of the table of legal characters.


Routines called:  None
Calling routines: EDIT, CREATE, SEE
Data areas accessed: XTABLE
Input parameters: FIELD -
Output parameters: RESU
ERROR conditions:  See
   od of operation
```

Fig. 3.4. Extract from a Coding Specification

require more levels of documentation with perhaps entirely different entries. For example, a compiler or translator would require quite complicated sections describing the source language accepted and the target object code for each source construct. These sections are essentially orthogonal to the sections on the structure of the compiler itself. Again design of an operating system involves the detailed documentation of very complex interactions and may well require an automated system, see reference 5).

The initial design strategy document incorporated standards, including the implementation language and other tools to be used, and other standards for coding and documentation were described in the PCD. Armed with these and the three levels of design document, coding begins after a design validation phase in which all members of the project and selected users are involved. The start of coding is heralded by a three-day talk-in for all project staff and invited guests to discuss the project, its design, the implementation plan and individual tasks.

In parallel with the design and coding activity the project manager has been considering integration and testing. He decides that unit testing, integration and system testing will be carried out by the production staff, and not separate teams, but appoints, early in the design stage, a senior member of the team to be an Integration and Quality Controller. This man is responsible for: specifying testing

46

INTERROGATION SYSTEM   QA1/IS/2

Test Strategies and Standards

Contents

1.   Introduction

2.   Test Strategy

      2.1   Unit Descriptions
      2.2   Function Testing
      2.3   Performance Testing
      2.4   Reliability Testing
      2.5   Interactions with Environment
      2.6   Standards

3.   Organisation of Testing

      3.1   Responsibilities
      3.2   Resources
      3.3   Tools
      3.4   Dependencies
      3.5   Documentation

4.   Impact on Design

5.   Impact on Coding

6.   Unit Test Specification Documents

7.   Integration Plans and Testing

Fig. 3.5. Contents List of Test Strategy Document

and integration strategy and standards, and for auditing these standards; organising a service team to assist the integrators; carrying out validation and user acceptance tests; and assisting the project manager during his day-to-day control of integration. The project manager and the controller together produce a testing strategy document: its contents list is Fig. 3.5. This covers the areas of testing needed for individual modules and subsystems, the way in which unit and system testing will be organised and the impacts on design, coding etc. It states the way in which those responsible for individual units must draw up test plans, and the controller assists with and approves these, and monitors progress against them. The controller also interacts with the designers and makes sure that his needs for measuring reliability and performance are taken account of in the design.

Staff responsible for testing modules and subsystems both individually and during integration are required to draw up a Test Specification document to a format set out in section 6 of the Overall Strategy document and to agree this with the controller. The specification document lists: the functions that are to be tested, how they should be checked and in what conditions; interfaces with other units and the system software and hardware; tests to be carried out for behaviour on error conditions; performance tests; and reliability measurements. From these, specifications for individual test programs are drawn up and attached as appendices, and plans for their production are incorporated into the over-all project plan to ensure the necessary resources are provided and timescales met. In addition to these individual test programs, some over-all test tools are found by the controller to be required, including a module test harness and an automatic results comparison program to avoid scanning reams of paper by eye. The controller produces a small scale FRS and PCD for these in co-operation with other project members and arranges for a sub-project to be set up to provide these items.

The controller next turns his attention to validation and acceptance testing and draws up an outline plan for these. This will be expanded later in the project but in the meantime he must at least obtain an agreement with the customer as to what will constitute acceptance of the system and what variances on full specification can be permitted. From this he derives an outline validation test and plans for the production of sufficient test material for this period. He negotiates the production of some of this with the users and arranges for field testing by one department before general release.

Close contact with the customer and the users has continued throughout this phase and the test material is not the only example of co-operation. Some of the designers have spent time in user departments to familiarise themselves with problems and needs, and arrangements have been made for user staff to assist in integration, validation and documentation. This contact has advantages for both parties.

Some time before integration begins, the project manager, helped by the controller, establishes the support team and produces a detailed plan which can be broken down to daily steps for a few days at a time. They decide to maintain an integration register on the computer itself in order to have up-to-date statistics accessible by all project members. The register is implemented simply as a text file held by the operating system and the computer manufacturer's editor is used to access and update it. The integration services team are responsible for maintaining this register which is kept very basic. An entry is shown in Fig. 3.6. Back-up information, such as the names of the functional tests not yet passed, are held by the person nominated responsible and a list of errors and restrictions referred to in the entry is held on another file.

```
MODULE NAME:  SRECRF
VERSION NUMBER:  38
MASTER COPY:    RJCLIB/1
RESPONSIBLE:  RJC

UNIT TESTS           TOTAL   RUN   SUCCESS   AS AT
FUNCTIONS              4      4       4      030574
PERFMNCE               1      1       1      050574
SYS VERS:  4                                 070574
FUNCTIONS              2      2       2      070574
INTERFACES             9      7       6      110574

  KNOWN RESTRICTIONS:    17,X61
KNOWN ERRORS       :   0
SUSPECTED ERRORS   :   SER7
```

Fig. 3.6. Module Integration Register Entry

The use of the computer for this purpose was a marginal decision but was taken because there was machine time available and it was considered useful to make the project team members take their own medicine. For a larger project the use of the computer might well have been essential but with a system of this size a wall display would almost certainly have been as effective. The computerised system does, however, provide a useful basis for a final user reference system once the product has been released.

4 Planning

There are three prime reasons for producing a plan. First, the act of planning causes the project manager to consider and allow for possible future problems. Second, the plan itself forms a basis for measuring progress and thus for control and future management action. Last, it provides an estimate of duration, required resources and cost for the project.

Plans may take many forms but there are a number of vital components which any plan must include:

- a list of activities.
- a list of resources needed at each stage.
- a logical relationship between the activities themselves and with any external dependencies.
- a list of assumptions.

The last is the most frequently forgotten, although at least as important as the others. It can cover a wide variety of things, from machine time availability through computing rates and impacts on others projects, to the start date of the implementation.

From these components the important outputs of the plan, the projected end date and the various aspects of the cost of the project can be derived. The method of presentation and recording of the plan is of secondary importance. For example the use of a computer-based PERT system should not necessarily be regarded as a good thing in its own right. It should be employed only if it aids the project manager in his control and reporting functions. This will normally be the case for large projects but even then it is necessary carefully to check the efficiency and availability of the PERT systems to ensure that the required rate of turnround for PERT updating and recording runs can be achieved. For smaller projects hand-drawn bar charts, networks and resource graphs may well be just as effective and less costly. However, in this case the manager must make sure that these documents are regarded as unchangeable without formal control, something that is much easier to do with a computer data base than with an A4 sheet.

4.1 Basic plans

An earlier section dealt with the production of an outline plan by the project manager as a basis for all further work. This plan should be kept simple: try to keep it down to 25 or so activities and certainly no more than 40. This number should be largely independent of the size of the project; larger projects will have less detail in their outline plans than smaller projects. At this stage the project manager should not attempt to consider the activities of individual project team members. Estimates should be based on average coding rates, average use of machine time per programmer and so on. Although the emphasis is on simplicity even the outline plan must include sections on activities, resources, relationships and assumptions.

The project manager should discuss the plan with, and have it vetted and agreed by, as many people as possible. Advice at this stage should always be welcomed even if not all of it is accepted. The most important people whose agreement is required are the customer, the project manager's own superiors and any subordinates who are already assigned to the project. It is perhaps most important that the assumptions are understood by these groups, since what appears reasonable to the project manager may not appear so to the people with wider, or narrower, horizons. These discussions may involve changes to the outline plan but perhaps more importantly they will identify the areas of greatest risk. These areas should be documented and kept up-to-date so that special management attention can be devoted to them. The project manager should also at this stage be able to place some limits of probability on meeting the complete plan.

Once the outline plan has been agreed it becomes the top-level plan for the project. Events on this plan become secondary objectives for lower level, more detailed plans. The number of levels of plan will depend on the size of the project and the project manager's own preferences but more than three is normally unmanageable, because of the problems of keep them in step. The lowest level must be of sufficient detail to allow each individual team member to see his own activities for the next few weeks. There is no need for lower-level plans to exist as a single document providing control is strong enough to ensure that the individual parts are compatible with the next level up. Again, although the top-level plan must cover the whole duration of the project, lower levels can cover progressively shorter periods of time and be updated on a rolling basis. If this is done the project manager should personally ensure that no individual ever runs over the end of his existing plan.

Production of lower level plans may well produce mismatches with higher levels. In this case mechanisms must be provided for iterating between the levels to bring them back into line. When lower-level plans are produced estimates for durations and resource requirements will be needed and must be reconciled with the higher-level estimates. The project manager must remember that it is bad for everyone concerned for him to have to reject outright a plan presented to him by a subordinate. For this reason it is often good practice to obtain best, worst and most likely estimates for lower-level plans, to leave room for discussion with the subordinate. If the project manager believes that estimates can be reduced he should attempt to convince the subordinate that this is so and to show him ways of carrying out the task in less time or with less resources. Only if the subordinate is convinced will he be able to commit to the new figures.

The project manager must be responsible for setting standards for planning and for satisfying himself that they are followed, but apart from the top-level plan the actual drawing up of plans should be done by the staff members concerned. The important points are that the project manager should be convinced that the plans are realistic and he should obtain commitment to the plans. Commitment to plans can only be obtained from individuals and the project manager should hold meetings with at least his immediate subordinates to obtain their commitment to their parts of the plan. He must also satisfy himself that the interactions between his subordinates are clear and capable of being monitored.

Just as lower-level plans may conflict with higher-level ones, the top level plan to which the project manager can obtain (and give) commitment may well not meet the requirements of the FRS and

53

. PCD. The project manager must first, of course, convince himself that the plan cannot be improved. He should look for, and remove, any unnecessary activities, especially in the tool area, where effort is being devoted off the main line of development. He should not however at this stage reduce his contingency margins or plan for such things as compulsory overtime or shift work. Again, under no circumstances should he arbitrarily cut individual timescales or resource estimates without producing new evidence to show that the change is feasible.

Once the project manager is convinced that the plan cannot be improved he must negotiate the mismatches with his user (or his superiors, or both) to obtain revised budgets or requirements. It is unwise to enter these negotiations with a bald statement of facilities to be dropped, expected lateness or budget overrun. The situation will rarely in practice be as simple as this and the customer, for example, will know much more about the relative importance of facilities than the project manager can. The project manager should discuss the problems with his staff to discover the possible tradeoffs that can be made. All these possibilities should be presented to the customer, although it is sensible for the project manager to recommend a particular choice of action. He should also welcome investigations of his plans and expose his unsuccessful attempts to meet the original requirements, since it is essential that there is an agreement between him and his customer on what is possible and what is not. Once the project manager has negotiated the necessary changes (or been genuinely convinced that the original requirements can after all be achieved) the plans must be altered accordingly and commitment to the new plans obtained from his subordinates.

4.2 Estimating

One of the major activities concerned with drawing up any plan is concerned with estimating the durations of activities and the resources required to carry them out. This has to be done by extrapolating on past experience and the accuracy of the estimate will depend on the availability and accuracy of historical data and the similarity of the conditions under which this data was collected to those that the present project will encounter. The viability of the plan is directly dependent on the reliability of the estimating process. It is therefore sensible to devote some time to establishing an estimating methodology which gives as much cross-checking as possible and places values on the reliability of estimates used. While it is by no means true that a plan is as reliable as its least dependable estimate, it is worthwhile bearing in mind that accuracy will vary and it is sensible to review those areas of low accuracy which lie on or close to the critical path at regular points throughout the project.

Aron (2) in his paper on estimating resources for large programming systems offers a number of different methods of estimating:

The Experience method. Comparing the new project (or sections of it) with similar previous ones, assuming that like tasks take like resources and applying factors for minor differences.

The Quantitative method. Basing estimates on the number of deliverable instructions or lines of code per average programmer per unit of time.

The Constraint method. The inverse of most methods, this essentially consists of determining the resources available and adjusting the specification to fit.

The Unit of Work method. Splitting the total task into independent activities each of four to eight weeks for one programmer.

Of these methods the experience method is undoubtedly the best, but depends on the existence of previous similar projects. It is particularly dangerous to use this method to extrapolate from small projects to large ones, since differences will be caused by interactions which had no parallel in the smaller project. The constraint method can only work in circumstances in which the users can accept the changes to specification, and delivery date is of paramount importance. Units of work are successful in small projects, particularly in commercial data processing, but require the project to be capable of resolution into discrete tasks; this is not possible for a large software system.

One is left therefore with the quantitative method as the main cross check for experience. Essentially one first estimates the size of the final system, applies factors to account for difficulty of the code

55

and the language to be used, and then using the duration of the project as a constraint and known production rates calculates the effort required. Aron gives some rates for use in these calculations and others may be found in the literature or, best of all, in the records of previous projects. Good standard values for such figures in a commercial environment, together with reliability factors, can be found in an excellent book on the subject produced by the Central Computer Agency (9).

While a formal approach to estimating is to be recommended, it is important for the estimator to question each of the parameters he uses and each of the results he obtains. It is particularly important to establish that figures are being used in the same context. For example, when using an estimate based on man-months, was it calculated using productive men, that is those actually coding, or gross men, including managers, operators, administrators, secretaries, etc.? Again, was account taken of the fact that usually only three-quarters of a team member's time is likely to be devoted directly to the project, the remainder going on holidays, training, sickness, etc. Was the effort expended on documentation (15 per cent of the total manpower on an average product) included or not? The important point is not that measurements should be made in a particular way but that the estimator should make sure that when extrapolating from past experience he is comparing like with like.

Less tangible factors will also have an effect on the accuracy of a comparison. For example, a team which has worked together before will normally be more productive (and more accurate in their predictions) than one that has not. All such factors should be taken into account. When total timescales and resources have been estimated they should be compared with as many previous projects as possible, even those which are only partially similar, and the project manager should attempt to explain any great differences in total figures or rates by known improvement areas or increased constraints or difficulties. If he cannot do this to his satisfaction further investigation is needed.

I mentioned earlier that it is difficult (and dangerous) to extrapolate from a smaller project to a larger one. The reason is of course that as the task becomes larger, the communication effort increases and in time tends to dominate the total effort required. Under such circumstances the addition of men-months to the resources produces diminishing returns and may, above some staffing level, even have a negative effect. Except on very small projects therefore the man-month should not be regarded as equivalent to a constant unit of output (see Brooks (7)).

In similar fashion, a machine hour is only a gross unit for measuring machine requirements. While the machine hours used per man-month will normally be fairly constant over similar projects, the amount of work done during a machine hour will vary greatly. To take a trivial example, during unit testing an hour a day for a week will normally be much more productive than four hours on a Sunday night, while during validation the reverse may be true. Again, the usage will depend critically on the turnround and mode of operation (batch or on-line). For this reason assumptions about the machine time availability must be included in the plan. They should be documented and available to whoever is providing the machine service if this is not under the project manager's direct control. The requirements will need to be up-dated regularly and should cover such items as operating environments, configurations, support needed from other projects, filestore requirements and media needed.

Finally, especially in the first planning stages, it is essential that the project manager fights for realistic schedules. When the estimating techniques are as primitive as they presently are for software, there is always a tendency to be optimistic and to tell the customer what he wants to hear. Remember that there is no real substiture for calendar time and a happy customer at the end of the project is a much better proposition than a happy customer at the beginning.

4.3 Dependencies

Dependencies between the project and other projects should be regarded as Bad Things and kept to an absolute minimum. Incoming items which are produced outside the project have the obvious disadvantage of not being under the project manager's control. This problem will not be solved by building in contingency periods between planned availability and the date when the incoming items are really needed, since the project manager will not be able to convince his suppliers of the urgency of his requirements until the contingency has been used up, and by then it may be too late. It may often be better to make use of an existing product than to depend on the production of a new one, however much the theoretical improvement may be. Items from the current project on which other projects depend have a different problem in that they complicate the objectives of the team: which is more important, meeting the dependency or progressing along the main path?

If it is impossible to avoid inward or outward dependencies, at least keep them off the critical development path and keep them constantly under review. The project manager should hold regular meetings with his suppliers or subsidiary customers and maintain a signed-off definition of exactly what constitutes the fullfilment of the dependency. It is worthwhile planning to lend staff to supplying projects to familiarise themselves with the product which will be delivered, in order to cut down the 'running-in' period when it is handed over. Similarly, the project manager should encourage secondments into his unit from 'customer' units for the same purpose.

In very large projects internal dependencies of a similar type may arise between different parts of the project. The project manager should encourage his staff to deal with these in a similar way, in particular demanding detailed definition of the dependency and interchange of staff for familiarisation.

4.4 Budgets, financial and other

Most project managers will be familiar with financial budgets and will recognise the need not only to meet total cost constraints but to keep within a phased budget throughout the project. The normal expenditure curve will be similar to Fig. 3.1. and it can easily be seen that a project which has spent half its money at the halfway point in time is almost certain to overrun. Equally, it is very unlikely that expenditure will double or halve from one month to the next, and no estimates should be based on such an assumption. A phased budget based on a smooth curve is a powerful tool for both financial control and financial forecasting. However, the basic idea of a budget can be used in many other areas to great advantage.

A simple example is given by staff numbers. The size of a team

should always follow a fairly smooth curve since a large step function is certain to cause dislocation and a fall in efficiency. A staff
budget curve should be drawn at the outset of the project and
recruiting (and staff transfer) pattern should follow this curve. If it
does not, then the curve must be redrawn without introducing
impossible slopes. If this cannot be done the whole plan will almost
certainly have to be renegotiated. In a similar way a phased machine
time budget can be built up and compared with both the staff
build-up and the over-all project resource curve of Fig. 3.1 for
consistency.

Less obvious, but of even greater importance, are performance
and facility budgets. If a large system has to provide a number of
facilities it is as unreasonable to expect all of them to be demonstrable for the first time in the last month, as it is for the financial
expenditure to halve in that month. It is therefore sensible to draw
up a budget for facility availability in the form of system milestones.
By this I mean that there should be at regular intervals, from the
start of integration to the beginning of validation, a demonstration
of the existing state of integration showing what new or improved
facilities are available. Since this is a prime control mechanism, it is
dealt with at greater length in the section on monitoring.

With all the budgets mentioned to date, where phasing is against
time, it is worthwhile to draw a graph of the relationship. If the
curve is not smooth or if it is very steep in places, it is unlikely that
the budget will be met. An example of a machine budget curve is
shown in Fig. 6.2.

Performance is an equally important facet of the project but has
no corresponding curve. Unhappily, a common method of dealing
with performance, for size, speed and reliability, is to:

1. Agree on reasonable targets at the start of the project.
2. Pay no further attention to them until the system is fully
integrated.
3. Measure the actual values.
4. Find a difference of a factor of ten or more.
5. Make frantic changes which improve at best by a factor of two,
while at the same time introducing errors and putting all the
documentation out of date.

59

6. Finally issue at a reduced specification and start a large and costly enhancement program to produce a new version which does meet the required targets.

This pattern can be avoided but only at the expense of a considerable amount of work during the early design phase, followed by monitored performance budgets. Essentially the requirements, which are analogous to total financial budgets, must be broken down into smaller units which can be controlled early in the program. A total size target for the final product must be divided up and assigned to individual modules as the detailed design proceeds. This budget then forms a part of the module specification.

Slightly more difficult is speed. During the design stage it is necessary to isolate critical paths through the system which are of importance to the design speed targets. These targets will normally be measured in terms of response time or throughput and the breakdown requires care to ensure that all critical paths are discovered and that reducing the length of one does not make a different path critical. Once this has been done maximum values in terms of instruction counts can be given to each element of each path and again this will become part of module specifications. Total system measurement will be needed during, and at the completion of, integration and it may still be necessary to tune paths that were overlooked in order to achieve the required performance. However with a performance budget it is unlikely that any very nasty surprises will be thrown up by the measurements and massive redesign is almost certainly avoided.

Reliability is even more difficult to control but needs to be approached in a similar fashion. Control of the size alone will reduce the number of bugs in the system itself since the error content to size relationship is normally much worse than linear. In addition, calculations can be done based on the reliability requirements and the projected speed to determine how often consistency checks, dumps, etc., are needed. Finally, as described earlier, this area must influence the testing strategy adopted.

5 Change control

All those concerned with a project plan, including all team members and the customer, must realise that it is bound to change in the course of time. While it is obviously good to have as few changes as possible, it is essential to make sure that all changes are made in a controlled and open manner and that the quality of the new plan is at least as good as the one it replaces. An out-of-date plan is worse than useless, since it means there is no common agreement on what is actually happening, and no means for the project manager to exert proper control. (To quote an extreme view from Robert Heller (6) in slightly different context 'don't forget (a) that any plan worth making is inaccurate; (b) that the longer a plan takes to write, the worse it is – just because of its consumption of time; (c) that the more [managers] change plans to suit events, the better they will manage – if you've made a mistake, you had better admit it'.)

Reasons for changes to plans may come from within the team and may be caused by new ideas or better understanding, as well as by failure to keep to schedule. Other reasons may come from outside in the form of changes to the objectives or the constraints. Major changes of this nature should produce an immediate replanning exercise, but it is worthwhile also to incorporate into the original plan specific review points at which the project manager and his team can stand back from the day-to-day activities and see what plan changes are needed. Such review points should be at about three month intervals for a project with a duration of a year or more and possibly more frequent for smaller projects.

When a replan is carried out it should cover the entire project and not just pieces of it. The replanning should be done to the same standards and principles as the original plan but should incorporate all the experience gained to date. The new plan should not be more complicated than the old one or its reliability will fall and the only result will be yet another replan soon. (To quote Brooks (7) 'Take no small slips'.) In particular the amount of parallelism should not be increased unless there are definite reasons for believing it is manageable; short fat networks should always be preferred to tall thin ones. Just as in the first plan, the project manager should try to meet all constraints or negotiate relaxations, and the new agreed

61

plan must be taken down through the levels and commitment obtained.

It is important that the changeover to the new plan is done simultaneously by all the team on the command of the project manager. While the new plan is being negotiated all project work and monitoring must continue against the old plan. This may cause some delay in theory but in practice to allow a phased changeover loses most of the project manager's control and should be avoided at all costs.

When a move is made to a new plan with the knowledge and agreement of all concerned, the old plan should be completely disregarded. However the project manager should keep all old plans, together with the reasons for their rejection, since they remain a vital part of the project history.

4.6 General planning points

This section is devoted to a number of general points which the project manager should bear in mind when planning or replanning.

- Never get yourself on the critical path. The project manager should regard himself as a reserve resource to chase, co-ordinate and rescue from disaster, never as a prime development resource.

- Try never to base new products on a new technology or new tools. This has the effect of squaring your uncertainties rather than doubling them. Use existing tools and technology wherever possible unless the benefits fully justify the risk of total failure.

- Use contingency in an open fashion. Contingencies should be put into a plan to cover the areas of greatest risk and should be clearly designated as such. Hidden contingencies inserted by inflating estimates, distort the plan and are almost certain to be used. Use of contingency should be only by permission of the project manager.

- Tread a realistic path between optimism and pessimism. A team will normally work best if they believe their schedules are difficult but not impossible: too easy and there is a Parkinsonian tendency to fill the time available; too difficult and they will consider it not worth even trying.

- Maintain contact with your customer throughout the project, but particularly when planning. Try to understand what he thinks his problems are and make sure he knows what you believe your problems, and his, are.

- Consider very carefully trade-offs which involve your ability to control. For example, commonality of sections of code between two contemporaneous projects will save overall costs (maybe!) but reduce the project manager's control over his project. On the other hand, standardisation of interfaces may allow similar flexibility in the future and actually increase the project manager's ability to control at the possible cost of reduced efficiency.

- Remember to allow for overheads, including:

  Learning time.

  Holidays and other lost time.

  Support to users and from suppliers.

  Putting right errors.

  Meetings, which rise as the square of the number of staff.

  Communications effort, which also rises as the square of the staff numbers, and is at least doubled if there is any geographical split among the team.

  Obtaining, checking and preparing test material.

  Implementation, testing and monitoring tools and utilities.

  Measurement runs.

  Organising use of machine time.

.7 Examples

For simple projects, or low-level plans of more complicated projects, a bar chart may be an adequate method of displaying the plan. It has the great advantage that it can be mounted as a wall display and one copy can therefore be kept which is on display to the whole project. A sample bar chart is shown in Fig. 4.1. It represents the lowest level of plan for a part of a project over a limited period. The initials of individual project staff are assigned to the bars which represent tasks. Members of staff may be concerned with one or more such tasks simultaneously. The numbers beneath the bars

63

STAFF	FEBRUARY			MARCH			APRIL		MAY			JUNE	
	6	6	6	11	11	6	4	5	5	3	3	3	1	0

DRS AJH — SR SCAN — SPECIFY 0 — CODE 16 — UNIT TEST 16 — INTEGRATE & SYSTEM TEST 18 — MKO base system available

DRS — MKI TESTING — ESTABLISH MKI TEST STANDARDS 0

AJH — VALIDATION SUITE A — DOCUMENT 0

RVW PWB KJB — TEST HARNESS — INTEGRATE & SYSTEM TEST 24 — VALIDATION 21

KJB — PRODUCE USER SPEC 0 — AGREE SPEC 0 — USER DOCUMENTATION — PRODUCE CATALOGUE AND ABSTRACTS 0

MACHINE TIME

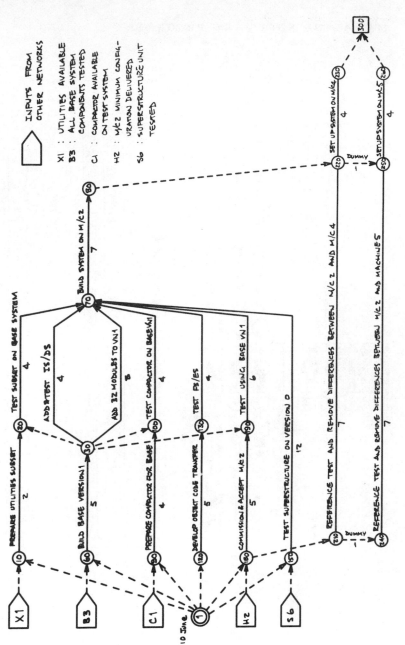

Fig. 4.2. An Integration Network

65

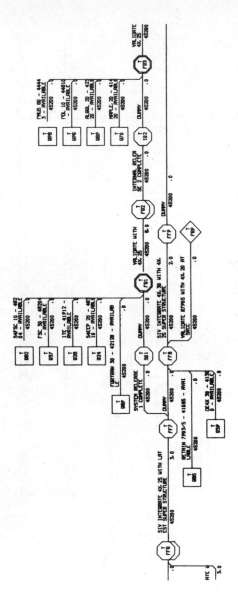

Fig. 4.3. A Computer-produced Network

Fig. 4.4 Sample PERT output

represent the estimated machine time needed for the activity. To a first approximation this is distributed evenly throughout the period of the activity and total machine requirements by week can be aggregated and are recorded at the bottom of the chart. This provides one of the assumptions made by the planner: that such time will be available; other more detailed assumptions are recorded elsewhere. There is only one external dependency for this section of the plan, which is shown by the arrow marked 'MK0 base system available'. Other internal dependencies are implied since movement of staff on to a new task presupposes completion of a previous one. In practice this break may not need to be as clean as the chart implies. The bar chart will be backed up by documents describing the tasks and their phases in detail and in particular specifying completion criteria. A bar chart of this type can be used in a fairly obvious way to record progress by marking the 'time now' point on the bottom scale and indicating the point reached on the tasks represented by the bars. This is particularly useful if the bar chart is a wall display.

In large projects, especially at higher levels of plan, the complexity of interactions tends to be too high to allow representation on a simple bar chart. Instead a network representation is needed. Fig. 4.2 shows such a network for the integration phase of a software system which has to be made available on three separate hardware systems. Each activity is represented as a solid line between numbered event nodes and the total task begins at event 1 on 10 June and ends at event 300. Dependencies from other networks are indicated and listed at the top right hand corner. Dummy activities, which are used to achieve the correct phasing of events, are indicated by broken lines and are assumed to have zero duration except where otherwide indicated, e.g. the non-zero dummy from event 210 to 240 ensures that the two reference test activities are staggered.

Since laying out such a network as this against a timescale line normally obscures the logic, estimated durations are marked in weeks under each activity line. From this it can easily be seen that, given that the external dependencies are satisfied, the critical path through the network from event 1 to event 300 is 25 weeks and passes through events 60, 30, 70, 80, 220, 250 and 260. Such networks are of course also capable of computer processing by

PERT packages and Fig. 4.3 shows part of a computer-produced network. Such packages will analyse critical paths through the network and calculate earliest and latest start dates for each activity, if given forecast durations. More complex packages can also calculate resource requirements and limitations. Fig. 4.4 is a sample of such output. It shows five activities and for each gives the numbers of the event nodes which begin and end the activity, the activity name, the estimated duration, earliest and latest start and finish dates and the 'float'. This last is the time by which the completion of the activity can slip without affecting the end date for the total project. The first few items shown have zero slip and are therefore on the critical path; the last activity has 15 weeks in hand before it shows an effect on the total end date.

Whether the computer is used or not for network recording and analysis, the network cannot by itself constitute a plan and requires to be supported by information on resources and assumptions together with detailed activity descriptions and completion criteria. The network of Fig. 4.2. for instance is backed up by a document which identifies:

- staff allocation to activities.
- software components required.
- a narrative description of the integration strategy.
- machine time requirements in terms of hours, turnround, times of day and levels of service.
- assumptions on overtime and weekend working.
- activity descriptions.

An example of the latter is found in Fig. 4.5.

Other documents go to make up the total plan, the most important being the budgets for resources. As stated earlier these are normally best represented as graphs whenever possible. The lower half of Fig. 6.2 shows a machine time budget represented as a histogram (the broken line) and most other resource budgets can be similarly drawn. In this case, as with the earlier activity bar chart the same diagram is being used to show actual 'expenditure' against the planned budget.

A performance budget on the other hand can only be produced as part of module or subsystem specifications by placing limits on

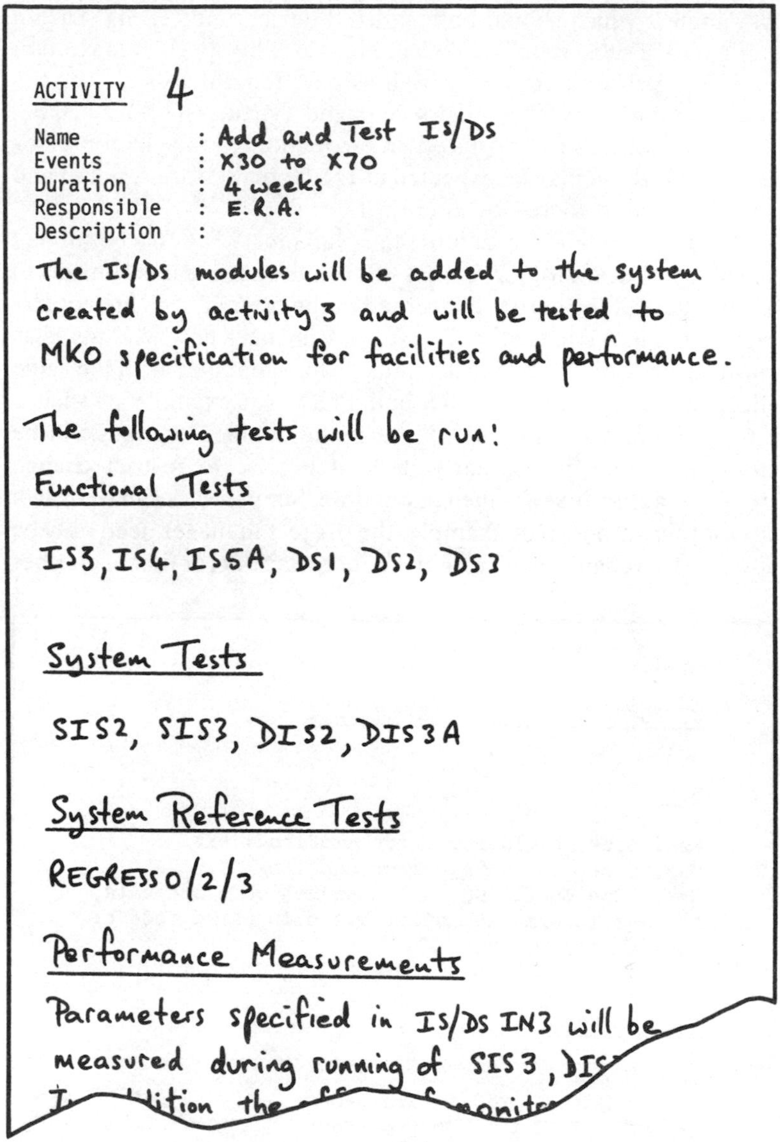

ACTIVITY 4

Name   : Add and Test Is/Ds
Events   : X30 to X70
Duration   : 4 weeks
Responsible : E.R.A.
Description :

The Is/Ds modules will be added to the system created by activity 3 and will be tested to MKO specification for facilities and performance.

The following tests will be run:

Functional Tests

IS3, IS4, IS5A, DS1, DS2, DS3

System Tests

SIS2, SIS3, DIS2, DIS3A

System Reference Tests

REGRESS 0/2/3

Performance Measurements

Parameters specified in Is/Ds IN3 will be
measured during running of SIS3, DIS
In addition the   monit

Fig. 4.5. An Activity Description

69

parameters which should be measured during unit testing. Such a budget for a subsystem is shown in Fig. 4.6. This specifies maximum code and private data size as well as path lengths. Also, since the implementation is planned for a paged (virtual store) machine, separate restrictions are placed on error coding, since in non-error conditions these may be expected not to be main store resident and their size is not therefore so critical.

All the items which constitute the plan must of course be subject to change control. Major replans will require special mechanisms to ensure that all the parties concerned in the original plan are equally concerned in the new plan. Day-to-day changes however, made as more information becomes available, can be handled with the same mechanism used for the FRS and PCD. An example of such a change is shown in Fig. 4.7. Since many detailed changes will be made especially in the early days, it is wise to restrict change approval authorities as much as possible. Simple rules can be drawn up for this purpose; for example, the project manager need only be involved if a change to an activity reduces its float (or that of another

```
PERFORMANCE BUDGET - MESSHAND 1


Size

Max. size, excluding error handling: 6Kb
Max. size, including error handling: 7.51Kb
Note: size to include all unshared code and data,
linkage information etc., but not shared code or
common data.


Path Lengths

Null message:   300 instructions
Simple SEE:     950 instructions
Com        EA: 1      structions
```

Fig. 4.6. A Performance Budget

INTERROGATION SYSTEM
LEVEL I NETWORK
CHANGE PROPOSAL

CP
NWI/IS/7   9

PROPOSED BY: J.V.B.

BRIEF DESCRIPTION OF CHANGE PROPOSED

Reduction of testing of BW subsystem under MK2 system to regression and confidence check only, at cost of increasing demo. version testing under MK0 and MK1.

REASON FOR PROPOSED CHANGE

- To reduce dependency on MK2 version
- To increase the total amount of testing to cover areas suggested by user contact (see IS/IN/71)
- To increase BW float from 1 to 4 weeks

APPROVAL OBTAINED   JS, ARB, DC.

DETAILED CHANGES

Network: Replace all activities between events B301 and B719 by attached network

Resources: Total machine time requirements unchanged but now phased as follows:
Ma   e 27

Fig. 4.7. Plan Change Proposal

71

activity) to two weeks or less. However it is vital that such agreements when made are recorded publicly and that the project manager is aware of them. The whole of his ability to control depends on his having a well understood plan against which any deviations can be brought to his notice immediately. More of this in a later chapter.

5 Organisation and staffing

This chapter covers the choices that can be made in the organisation
of a software development team and the way in which staff should
enter and operate within the chosen organisation. It considers first
the way in which the project manager fits in with his team, which is
the most fundamental choice to be made, and then goes on to look
at more detailed operating aspects.

.1 The project manager and his team

The project manager can take up one of three relationships with the
rest of the team. In each case he must be concerned with both the
administrative aspects of management and the technical viability of
his project, but the balance can vary. The three possibilities are:

- primarily an administrative manager, monitoring the technical
  aspects.
- administrative manager and technical leader of the project.
- 'chief programmer'.

The first of these is perhaps the most common. The project
manager organises the team, approves plans and negotiates with the
customer but leaves detailed technical design and implementation
decisions to other members of the team. He must, however, satisfy
himself that the technical problems are being solved correctly and
consistently within the over-all requirements of the plan, and for
this purpose it is common for the project manager to have a 'chief
technician' responsible for the over-all integrity of the product.

The second type of organisation requires a project manager with
a detailed technical background, who besides managing the team, is
personally responsible for at least the outline design of the product,
and considers himself as the final arbiter on design decisions. With a

73

large team (say 15 or more) such a manager may require administrative assistance to help him with the day-to-day handling of the team, since a large part of his time will be taken up with technical matters.

The chief programmer approach takes this one stage further. As described by Baker (8), this organisation involves the project manager being the chief designer and implementor of the project, who parcels out parts of his work to the other team members on almost a sub-contract basis. The chief programmer has a backup programmer to assist him and administrative work is delegated to another team member. This form of organisation is dependent on the adoption of top-down design and structured programming. The productivity and quality of output quoted for the few documented examples of the use of this technique are outstanding (e.g. 7500 lines of high-level source code delivered per man year, first error found in a file processing system after 20 months of use).

The choice between these methods will depend on many things. Most important, of course, is the experience and inclinations of the project manager himself, but the size of the project and the calibre of the staff are also significant factors. The chief programmer team is, without doubt, a particularly effective method, but depends on a project leader with a relatively rare mixture of skills and a small but highly competent team. In choosing both the method and the administrative or technical assistance required, the project manager should consider the amount of his time that will be taken up with such things as interfaces with his customers, his suppliers, if any, and his boss; regular administration activities; personnel matters; cost control; and inevitable crisis fighting.

Whichever organisation is adopted the project manager must realise that he always remains responsible for both technical and general management matters although he may choose to delegate some aspects of one or the other.

5.2 Team size

It is commonly believed that a large product requires a large team. While this is not necessarily so, the converse is always true: a large team will produce a large product. If at all possible the desired size

74

and structure of the final product should be determined first and the team organisation should reflect this, rather than the converse. As a general rule, the smaller the team the better, since the communication effort is kept to the minimum and direct productivity per member increases. The major disadvantage of a small team is its vulnerability to turnover. This can be guarded against by organising the team in pairs of senior and junior staff. The junior man then receives automatic on-the-job training and becomes a potential substitute should the senior man be lost.

Management limitations and the possible span of control will also place contraints on team size. The number of direct subordinates that the project manager can deal with successfully will depend on his relationship with his team. In general more 'administrative' relationships can be handled than 'technical' ones. Ten subordinates is probably a good limit over-all but this could fall to five if the normal communication is of a detailed technical nature or if the project manager is involved in detailed technical negotiations with his colleagues. The manageable span of control places direct limitations on the team size because the project manager should avoid the alternative of multi-levelled hierarchies of control in a software project. Such an organisation is not conducive to the rapid interchange of technical information or to rapid raising of technical problems for high-level decision.

With a small team a great deal of information will be exchanged during coffee and meal breaks. This forms an effective means of communication on both matters of general awareness and specific importance. In larger teams individual members should be encouraged to talk over their problems with each other. They should particularly discuss decisions which may affect other people directly with the people concerned, rather than writing memos to each other. Such communication is faster and more effective but carries with it the danger that important decisions may not be recorded or communicated to other interested parties. All staff should therefore be persuaded to document immediately any important decision reached at any formal or informal meeting and to register it in the project documentation. 'People to people' is a better communication method than 'paper to people'; 'people to people to paper' is better still. Again with a large team individual members often lose sight of the over-all objectives and progress of the project. Regular seminars help to keep a large team in touch with what is going on and are a reasonable substitute for small team coffee breaks.

Whatever size of team is chosen it is of paramount importance that in the event of project slippage the project manager does not attempt to make up time by increasing the size of his team. Brooks (7) coins the term 'Regenerative Schedule Disaster' for the well-known tendency to throw in more men, and goes on to state Brooks' First Law: 'Adding manpower to a late software project makes it later.' The disruption caused by such additions, coupled with the increased communication effort required will certainly make the situation worse. More men can never be regarded as a substitute for calendar time.

5.3 Recruiting

The effectiveness of the project team can be greatly affected by the way in which the members are recruited. In the general case, unfortunately, the project manager does not have complete control over this since he may inherit a ready-made team who are either in the process of finishing off another project, or have finished and are waiting for new work. Both these situations hold considerable problems which the project manager does not necessarily have the means to solve. This section deals with an ideal situation, which may well not be realisable, where the project manager is in complete control of recruiting. In practice, he must map his recruiting and staff build-up on to the ideal as best he can within whatever constraints are placed upon him.

It is obviously beneficial if the project manager can choose his own team, especially his immediate subordinates, since commitment on both sides will be much easier in such circumstances. It is also a good idea wherever possible to use an existing team for a new project providing their previous project was not so disastrous as to demoralise them completely or build up bad relations within the team. The ability to work together and communicate effectively is expensive to obtain and should not be lightly thrown away.

Within this framework, if at all possible, staff should be brought into the team only as work becomes available for them; the devil find work for idle hands and you may wind up with an unnecessarily complex project. It is wise in the early planning stages to build up a schedule of staff recruitment showing where each new job begins and when the job holder will need to begin familiarisation. The project manager must make sure that all new staff know both the objectives of the project as a whole and of their part of it. With large projects it is probably worth while to run a short course to show where everything fits in. If at all possible recruiting should be top-down, so that senior members can in turn train and familiarise more junior staff.

With regard to the placement of individuals, two extremes should be avoided: there should not be such detailed job descriptions that individuals are forced to fit them, regardless of their abilities or interests; neither should the individuals available determine the jobs. Job descriptions before recruitment are certainly to be recommended but they should be produced in broad enough terms to allow flexibility to meet individuals' needs.

If, through circumstances beyond his control, the project manager finds himself with more junior staff than he needs in the early stages of the project, he must plan carefully to utilise their time. The aim should be to find them real work to do which will prevent boredom but will not interfere with the design work going on, or take up too much of the senior staff members' time in control and advice. The best type of work is that off the main product development line such as constructing or collecting test material for debugging, validation or acceptance tests. Similarly such staff can spend some time familiarising themselves with the tools they are to use or working with the customer to obtain a 'feel' for the users requirements. Detailed allocation of tasks in the main project should be left as late as possible to avoid a Parkinsonian build-up.

When tasks are actually assigned they should be described in detail for each individual. Each individual team member should have available for reference:

● his own objectives.

● a schedule or network for his activities.

● a definition of completion criteria for his task(s).

● a list of assumptions and constraints.

One final point. When choosing staff for a project it is important to remember that attributes which are virtues at the development stage when recruiting begins, may turn to vices at a later stage. To quote Kinslow (1), there is a type of system designer who, if given five problems 'will come back and announce that these aren't real problems and will eventually propose a solution to the single problem which underlies the original five. This is the "system type" who is great during the initial stages of design of a project. However, you had better get rid of him after the first six months if you want to get a working system.'

5.4 Functional organisation

An earlier section recommended that the organisation of the team should reflect the structure of the product. To carry this to extremes one could have a subgroup of the team concerned with each component throughout all its design, coding, integration and testing stages. An alternative, but equally extreme, organisation would be to have separate elements responsible for each stage of production for all the components. In practice any organisation will be a compromise, and the most workable is probably a component-based organisation with some functionally specialised staff to provide co-ordination and standardisation across components. In particular it is almost always unwise to have a design/code split since all good designers should be tempered by hard implementation experience. It is better to 'grow' the design team into an implementation team by adding programmers to each individual designer and having the designer directly involved in the coding and subsequent stages (a chief programmer project automatically ensures this sort of operation).

In making his own compromise the project manager should bear in mind in particular the problems of communication within his total team. The grouping of sub-units within the team should be, if possible, such as to reduce the interactions between them, particularly with regard to the supply of tools, code or services. It is often worthwhile to represent the interactions diagramatically to spotlight the traffic of this type that goes on. It is also important that the members of any subgroup have similar objectives and work to the same sorts of time-scales. This will prevent difficult trade-off decisions at low level and ensure that they are raised to a point at which a total project view can be taken.

Organisation will also be affected of course by personnel considerations: individuals' skills, desires and experience. While very important, such considerations should be used to modify an ideal technical organisation rather than be the first consideration. The method in which the computer is used will affect the organisation in a similar way. For example, the amount of machine time available, the system operated and the access allowed may determine whether each member of the team should be responsible for his own machine usage or if runs should be co-ordinated and carried out by a specialised group. Similarly, if the project manager actually has control of a computer, rather than using a service provided by someone else, he may choose either to create his own service team within the project team or to integrate operators into the team itself to give them a better feeling of involvement.

One last area to be considered is that of administrative assistance. There will be much non-technical work within the project, particularly in the early stages; drawing plans, maintaining internal documents, producing reports and so on. These activities are very necessary but also very time-consuming, particularly in a large team, and the project manager must consider the most effective way of getting them done. If more staff are available than the ideal build up requires, it may be possible to use junior technical staff to do these jobs in the early design stages until their regular job becomes available. However, a specific non-technical clerical assistant can often be easily justified for a large project.

6 Monitoring and control

One of the reasons for drawing up a plan is to form a basis for measuring progress. This enables the project manager to pin-point problems as, or hopefully before, they arise so that he can take avoiding action. As we have seen, such action may involve replanning and the project manager must steer a careful course between constant crises caused in an attempt to hold to an unrealistic plan and constant replanning. His aim should be to hold to a plan for as long as it represents a course of action leading to a just-achievable target. To do this he needs advance warning of potential problem areas to allow him to manage around them. On the other hand he should devote much less of his time to areas which are going well. The reporting structures within the project should therefore be set up on a 'management by exception' basis.

The other important point to note is that while individual tasks on the plan will be delegated, the interactions between such tasks remain firmly in the project manager's hands. He must ensure that he has the means of monitoring these interactions. This chapter looks at techniques for monitoring the project against an agreed plan.

6.1 Milestones

One of the greatest difficulties with software projects is that, unlike building a house, for example, there is no measurable entity (like number of bricks laid) which has a direct relationship to the point reached in project plan. This leads to the '95 per cent finished syndrome' where the project is declared at regularly spaced reporting points to be 20 per cent finished, 40 per cent finished, 60 per cent finished, 80 per cent finished, 95 per cent finished, 95 per cent finished, 95 per cent finished, etc.

The only answer to this is to create events at regular intervals throughout the plan whose achievement can be demonstrated. Such milestones should be, as far as possible, genuine steps towards the end product. In some cases a degree of artificiality may have to be introduced, for example construction of a system with almost no facilities simply in order to demonstrate it. Such distortions do undoubtedly add to the total work done during the lifetime of the project but if the milestones are carefully chosen this increase can be easily justified in the light of the increase in control afforded to the project manager. The cost is akin to the difference between buying a second-hand car unseen or paying (at most) 5 per cent more in order to test drive it first.

The milestone events should be entered in the top-level plan and their existence and meaning should be known to all members of the project team. The frequency of the milestones is a matter for the individual project manager's judgement since he must balance the work to be done to demonstrate the milestone against his need to be regularly and reliably informed about progress. Something between six weeks and two months is a reasonable choice for a medium-sized project. It is worth while to have a short semi-formal demonstration of the system when a milestone is reached to which all members of the team are invited as well as the customer and possibly other future users. The aim of such a demonstration is not to prove that the event has conclusively been achieved (anyone who has organised demonstrations knows how easy they are to rig!) but to concentrate the efforts of the team members on to these regular sub-goals and to keep the customers in the picture of over-all progress.

A chosen milestone should be as far as possible a total system step. By this I mean it should include as many elements of the final system as possible, even if the facilities of these elements, or their performance, is very restricted. Since it is the construction of the total system from its 'working' component parts which is likely to give the most problems, and for which it is most difficult to measure progress, this is the area requiring the earliest possible demonstration. To give an example, if the product is a compiler the provision of a version which is capable of compiling only a null program is a better milestone than a syntax analyser capable of processing any program thrown at it.

81

On a larger scale if the product is a total control system with utilities and applications programs, there will be a strong tendency for individual subproject teams to test their own products independently for as long as possible. In this way they do not get involved with the problems of other products, or interactions between the two, which will appear to slow down their individual progress. In practice this merely delays the problems of integration to a later time by when they may well be more difficult to solve, and certainly the project manager will have less contingency to deal with them. Milestones in such a situation should be such as to cause the construction of a Mark Zero version of the total system as soon as preliminary versions of the individual elements exist. Such milestones may well involve advancing the 'natural' date of the start of integration; this can do nothing but good.

Again milestones should not be concerned solely with the progressive availability of facilities of the final system. Other areas of vital importance to the acceptability of the final system are sizes, path lengths, speed and reliability, all items to which budgets should have been assigned in the plan. At a system milestone the actual values corresponding to specific budget parameters in each of these areas should be measured and an advance estimate should be made by the team of the values they should be if the final target is to be met. This will ensure that problems in these areas are highlighted while there is still time to solve them, rather than at the last moment when the full system finally comes together. In order to measure the actual parameters, hardware and software monitoring tools will need to be available early in the over-all program.

Fig. 6.1 shows the contents lists and the start of the first section of a system milestone description. The first section goes on to describe in detail the user facilities available, wherever possible in the form of restrictions on the total functional description of the final system. This is followed by a section which describes the components which are used to build the system version, their version numbers and the documentation which describes them. The third section describes the level of testing which must be complete in order to meet the milestone. At an early stage in producing the milestone plan this will merely list functions to be available, speed and size parameters to be measured and reliability statistics to be collected. As the milestone approaches these will be extended by the names and version num-

BASIC TEST SYSTEM   MILESTONE
                                        S2

System Milestone Description

Mark 0

Contents

1. Description of Milestone
2. System Components
3. Testing Level

    3.1 Functional tests
    3.2 Performance measurements
    3.3 Reliability measurements

4. Documentation and support

5. Demonstration

1. Description of Milestone

This milestone represents the first total construction of
the Basic Test System. All major components are integrated
and all major user facilities are demonstrable but dummy
versions of the error handling routines and early, restricted
versions of I/O and formatting modules are incorporated, and
file handling is limited to built in system files.

User functions which can demonstrated are:

1. Edit N
2. SEND

Fig. 6.1. A Milestone Description

bers of specific test programs, both for individual components and
the total system, and targets for performance and reliability
parameters. The fourth section on documentation is important
since, unless the milestone is completely artificial, the system
created will be used later in project stages. It must therefore be well
enough documented for this purpose and will need to be supported
both by assigning responsibility to individuals to assist users and
arranging for procedures for error reporting etc. The final section,
which is completed fairly close to the forecast milestone date,

83

describes the demonstration which will be run for the team and invited users.

A significant advantage of the evolutionary approach of providing systems milestones is that a fallback is automatically provided in the case of disaster. Since some form of system exists from an early point in the project life it is almost certain that the last milestone systems before the first release will show sufficient resemblance to the complete product to allow one of them to be used instead of the final version, if that is delayed. Without a system milestone approach, hurried construction of such a fall-back when the slip is recognised usually produces a poor fall-back and disrupts the main-line development sufficiently to delay the final product even more.

Reaching a system milestone is also a good opportunity for examining the other resource budgets to see if they are following the curve which underlies the basic planning assumptions or whether some redistribution, or possibly renegotiation, is necessary. Finally, if there are any external dependencies in the project plan the project manager in his guise as customer should try to persuade his supplier to adopt a milestone approach and to phase his milestones to the needs of the supplied project.

6.2 Monitoring techniques

For the project manager to be able to control the project it is essential that he has up-to-date information on the current state of progress at all times. While the milestones provide well-defined steps in the total progress they will need to be supplemented by other progress reporting mechanisms. It is important that the information generated for this purpose should arise as far as possible naturally from the work of the team and not as a separate exercise. Regular written progress reports, or progress review meetings, have a tendency to generate a high overhead-cost-to-information-passed ratio and their effectiveness should be critically reviewed. More important is for the project manager to have early warning of possible crises. He should agree with his subordinates that he will be alerted immediately a possible crisis is identified. This, of course, runs counter to a normal human tendency to try to solve problems before bringing them up to a superior, by which time

84

it may be too late for the superior to help. The project manager must make a deliberate effort to make all project staff aware that a potential crisis alert is infinitely better than an actual crisis without advance publicity. He must also be very careful to be seen to help when an alert is raised rather than merely castigating those responsible for inefficiency. Such alerts are best tied to achievement of the next milestone event since this has an immediate impact and prevents the fatal assumption that it will all come right in the end. Alerts should be raised if the forecast date for the next milestone slips by more than amount determined by the project manager, or if projected performance will be worse than some specified percentage, or if financial or other budgets are exceeded by some margin, etc. Alerts should be presented in a standard fashion, together with the information the project manager is likely to need in order to take action himself. They should, for instance, state the problem, the effect of not remedying it on the end product, any actions already taken to put the situation right, any actions needed from other parties, possible solutions and a recommended solution if there is one.

An alert system will give the manager immediate information about immediate problems. Since the essence of control is based on forecasting the future it is also necessary to monitor trends. A financial spend or a code size which has been increasing exponentially over the last few months is unlikely to settle down without some specific corrective action and this action is almost certainly necessary regardless of the actual value of the parameter. Since the adoption of a budget technique and system milestones is aimed at providing as far as is possible a numerical assessment of progress, such trends can normally be best displayed as graphs or charts of one sort or another. Just as a picture is worth a thousand words, a graph is worth innumerable lectures about the need to curb optimism in forecasts.

For parameters subject to a budget constraint the method of recording can be a simple histogram plotting actual values against the original projection at regular stages, through the project. Fig. 6.2 shows an example of this type of graph for a machine time budget. The planned machine usage is shown as a broken line in the bottom diagram and this is checked for approximate consistency with the curve of Fig. 3.1. As the project proceeds actual achieve-

85

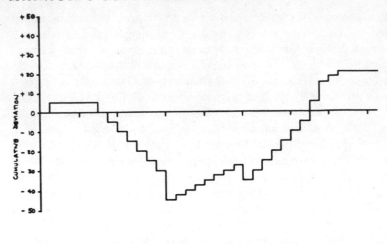

MACHINE USE GRAPHS

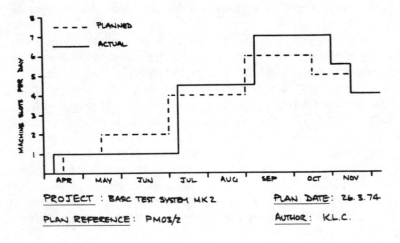

PROJECT : BASIC TEST SYSTEM MK 2   PLAN DATE : 26.3.74

PLAN REFERENCE : PM03/2   AUTHOR : K.L.C.

Fig. 6.2. Machine Time Graphs

ment is recorded on the same chart and in addition a cumulative deviation from the plan is also recorded on the upper chart. This record is particularly useful for displaying trends; while the mismatch of the solid and broken lines on the bottom chart does not

86

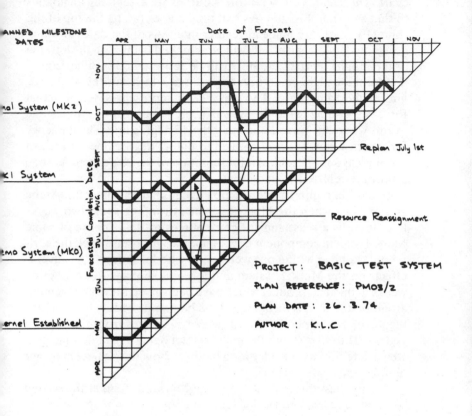

Fig. 6.3. A Slip Chart

look too alarming, the upper chart shows by the end of June a
potentially dangerous situation which the project manager must
take steps to put right. Recordings of this type can be applied to
code size, performance, financial spend, response times, staff numbers, machine time, average turn round times and numbers of runs.
Such charts help pinpoint problem areas or deviations from original
planning assumptions and allow action to be taken in time.

87

The equivalent of the histogram for timescale control is the slip chart. This can take several forms but all are essentially analogous to that shown in Fig. 6.3. As real time passes (along the top of the chart) forecasts are made at regular intervals of the dates at which designated milestone events will be achieved (shown on the left side of the graph). Perfect progress will be represented by a horizontal line from the planned date on the left axis which cuts the 45 degree line at the same date. The wavy lines represent a set of actual forecasts ending with the actual achievement of the milestone events where the forecast lines cut the 45 degree line. The tendency for forecast lines to crawl parallel to the 45 degree line for the last few forecasts is a graphical representation of the 95 per cent finished syndrome referred to earlier.

Two other points of interest are indicated on the diagram. At the end of May, when the Mark 0 system is running some two weeks late, there is a reassignment of resources at the expense of some Mark 1 system component development. This brings back the earlier milestone to within one week of its scheduled date. The adverse effects on the Mark 1 system and forecast slippage of up to three weeks in the final product which have been given little management attention till now, is recovered at the beginning of July by a replanning exercise helped by the release of resources from the Mark 0 system. The chart shows the final product being available some two weeks late. Let us consider for a moment how the project manager handles the reassignment.

The forecast three week slip in the Mark 0 system at the second week in May leads to the leader of the integration team raising an alert, two weeks having been previously specified by the project manager as the maximum permitted variance against a date target. Fig. 6.4 is a copy of the alert document which formally notifies the project manager, although he is simultaneously given the details personally. The project manager discusses the problem immediately with the integration team leader and then requests some further items of information from both the integration team and other project staff, ready for a meeting the following morning. Fig. 6.5 shows some extracts from his diary over the period of the alert.

The meeting is attended by all the Mark 0 integration team, senior staff from other areas of the project and two outside parties.

DATE ALERT   ALERT NO.
BASIC TEST SYSTEM   3
                          14.5.74

Problem
  Mark 0 (Demo System) is forecast 3 weeks
late against planned date of 1.7.74

Reasons
- Late handover of components MT3L, BASE2
- Possible forecast delay to establishment of Kernel
- Underestimate of machine time for test runs

Effects
Network shows direct effect on Mk2 system of 3
weeks of which 1 week probably recoverable in September.

Actions Taken
- Integration team working as two shifts to extend
attendance to 12 hour day
- Restricted system built using dummy versions
of MT3L, BASE2

Possible actions to recover slip
- PM to authorise weekend working
- PM to increase machine allocation during
weekday time
- Reduce specification of Demo System to
omit missing components

                       E. H.
                   14 May 74

Fig. 6.4. A Milestone Slippage Alert

14 May	Alert 3 raised : MKO milestone 3 weeks late. Discussed with EH
15 May	9.00 A3 meeting No 1 MKO team, seniors, ABT, WM 1. Kernel <u>not</u> a problem 2. ABT says no more week M/c time, some free at weekends. Authorise W/E working. <u>Action</u> EH to produce man and expenditure plan for using W/E time. 3. <u>Action</u> VP, BE to assess effect of transfer of weekdy allocation to MKO. 4. <u>Action</u> WM to assess effect of slipping MT3L, BASE2
21 May	AR3 meeting No 6 1. Forecast slip reduced to 2 weeks 2. Mk1 critical phase: no withdrawal of resources until after integrating base, forecast 1 June. 3. Mk2 machine allocation held, excess → MKO 4. <u>Action</u> BE to produce draft replan by June 14
7 June	MKO zero slip reported Alert 3 withdrawn

Fig. 6.5. Project Manager's diary of an Alert

The first of these latter is a representative of the computer service which the project uses for development. The total allocation of the machine time is under their control although the project manager can use his own allocation as he pleases. It is fairly obvious from initial discussions that more machine time would help and the project manager has already asked the integration team to draw up a table of the effects on their schedules of various increases in machine access. The other outsider is the customer. Although he is not actually going to use the Mark 0 version, any decisions taken may affect the final product and it is necessary to keep him informed. He may also be able to provide useful priority information from a customer point of view.

The project manager first satisfies himself that the reasons given for the slip are the true ones and do not conceal others. The fear about delay to the kernel is shown to be ill-founded: this milestone will complete on time. The other two reasons are valid and of these the machine time is the most vital. The computer service representative confirms that in the short term no extra time can be made available during the week but some is available at weekends. The project manager therefore immediately authorises weekend working within strict financial controls. This will not, however, solve the machine time problem and some reassignment will be necessary within the project. Components of the Mark 1 system are currently slightly ahead of schedule and Mark 2 is forecast on time. The integration managers for these system milestones are asked to assess the effect on their timescales of giving up the extra time needed by the Mark 0 operation. Quick responses are required next day with more detailed reports later. The customer is asked to assess the effect of slipping the two late components out of the demo system. He reports back the next day that one, MT3L, is not important but the other is so fundamental that he would be unhappy to see its integration left until a later milestone. Changes are made to the milestone content on these lines.

The first alert meeting lasts two to three hours. Subsequent meetings are held daily by the project manager but for approximately half an hour and not necessarily with all the original attendees. At the end of a week another full meeting is held, by which time weekend working and dropping MT3L have reduced the forecast slippage to two weeks. Although this is now within the permitted variance, the alert continues until the situation is seen to be under control. The Mark 1 system is itself entering a critical phase and it is decided not to attempt any resource reassignment until the first week in June. It has been established however that economies can be made in the later stages of Mark 2 work. Planned extra machine time for the Mark 2 system due in May is therefore diverted to the Mark 0 system (together with one member of staff, since with all this machine time men have become a limiting factor) and a replanning exercise for Mark 2 and the latter part of the Mark 1 system is set in motion with a target date of 1 July.

The effect of these actions can be seen from the Fig. 6.3 slip chart. By the first week in June Mark 0 is back on target, Mark 1 has been marginally adversely effected, while Mark 2 gets steadily worse against the existing plan, raising its own alert by the end of the month, and only coming under control with the completion of the replan. Daily meetings on Mark 0 continue until the alert is withdrawn.

This little history illustrates several points. First, the early raising of the alert helped the integration manager since it made available to him resources not previously under control. Second, the project manager took immediate control on a day-to-day basis from the moment the alert was raised and did not release his hold until he was satisfied that the integration manager was capable of carrying on. Third, all relevant parties were immediately involved. This is especially important for the customer since not only was he able to help, but direct involvement stopped him from forming the impression that he was being cheated out of something. Fourth, although he had set the replanning exercise in motion by the end of May, the project manager insisted on work to, and reports against, the old plan until the new one had been fully agreed, in order to retain his over-all control. Finally, for his records the project manager keeps details of actions taken, decisions taken, and reasons. He will also retain slip charts even when plans have changed so as to invalidate them completely. This data will certainly be of value in other projects to improve his forecasting, and may even be useful in the later stages of this project.

The alert system is of course only one monitoring method. As a general principal, the project manager should employ as many methods of cross-checking as possible without creating a secret police unit. The idea should be not to obtain information by means other than direct reporting, but to improve the reliability of the information that is reported directly. Thus desk checking of code by other programmers is a very cost-effective way of improving reliability and reducing timescales, and cross-checking plans and estimates increases their reliability. The best form of cross-checking is if some parts of the total product can be used as development tools by other parts. This gives the closest possible simulation of genuine usage, long before the first release.

Finally, remember that one of the project manager's greatest enemies is unjustified programmer optimism (see 7). Get staff to justify any estimates they are called on to make and use any means you can to make them realists. Remember, for example, that the questions 'when will you finish?' and 'when can I cut your machine time?' often produce very different answers!

.3 Resolution and review

Regular control activities should involve the minimum number of people at any one time. The project manager should remember that the loss of his subordinates' time attending large-scale regular review meetings is almost certainly more expensive than the extra time he personally spends in holding several smaller meetings. Providing he ensures that any actions of general interest arising from individual meetings are formally promulgated, the latter approach is more effective. On the other hand, on a large project a full-scale review involving all sections of the team is beneficial at widely spaced intervals. This is not because the project manager is likely to get more information from such a review but because it provides a method of bringing individual staff up to date on over-all progress and shaping the objectives for the coming period.

Another reason for a large-scale review is when a crisis occurs. In this case a resolution meeting can be held to determine what steps can be taken to recover, since it may be possible for the recovery action to be outside the immediate area in which the crisis becomes apparent. Such a meeting should be of fixed duration and the project manager should fight any attempt on the part of the members of such a meeting to perpetuate themselves as a regular review

93

body. Those present should address themselves purely to the immediate problem and should aim to come up with an agreed course of action at the end of the meeting. If no consensus can be agreed the project manager should rule, arbitrarily if necessary. It is very important to team morale that such reviews should appear to be decisive and it is in many cases better to decide now and change later than to delay a decision. In extreme cases where it is necessary to carry out some further investigation to determine the best of several courses of action, the project manager should commission such work but place a firm timescale on it and give a date for his decision.

As an alternative to a review meeting in the case of a crisis, or as a monitoring device, the project manager can establish an audit team to investigate progress or technical detail. Such a mechanism should not be used too often since it has a tendency to encourage hostility and its objectives and terms of reference should be well defined. An audit should be activated when needed and not be a planned regular occurrence. The auditors should be chosen at the time rather than having a pre-nominated audit team. Such audits do normally unearth problems earlier than they would appear of their own accord and thus allow more time to circumvent them. They also have the effect of getting the group being audited to think more about where they are and what they need to do, and give staff a chance to express their fears and problems without seeming to admit failure to their immediate superiors.

It will often be the case that an audit will be carried out in an area of the project in which there is an actual or potential failure, while the auditors will be drawn from more successful areas. In such a situation there will always be a temptation to allow the successful auditors to take over all or part of the ailing area. This temptation should be resisted because of the undoubted problems such a take-over always causes. Instead, the audit should be regarded as a co-operative venture between the auditors and auditees; they should both discuss any report before it is published and the original team must implement any corrective actions recommended.

Any review or audit should always consider first the objectives of the area under review and their relationship with the over-all project objectives. In a large project, goals chosen for subprojects can easily become distorted by emphasis on particular aspects to the

94

point where they are no longer in tune with the over-all project objectives. An audit or review is a good time to check the objectives for consistency and alter them if necessary.

Whatever reviews are held during the life of a project it is always advisable to hold a full-scale review at the end. A report should be produced which is given to all members of the team as well as being archived for posterity. Such a report should cover two main areas: summaries and lessons learned. The summaries should merely pull together the useful data which has been recorded throughout the project and put it in a sensible form for future estimating purposes. They should include machine usage figures, production rates, forecasts against achievement and so on. Lessons are rather more subjective. This section should certainly include details of all standards, techniques, and tools adopted, whether they were in practice reckoned to be good or bad, and why. More difficult, but equally important, is to attempt to record all the major decisions taken during the project, their effect and their effectiveness. Here it is useful to canvass all the team for suggestions, since decisions considered minor by the project manager may in practice have a considerable effect on coders two levels down.

7 Documentation

Documentation is an often neglected and delayed aspect of a software project which is nevertheless vital to success. Within well-run projects it is common for documentation of all sorts to account for about 15 per cent of the over-all project costs. This percentage should remain fairly constant throughout the project so the resources devoted to documentation should themselves follow the now familiar Fig. 3.1 curve.

Documentation forms a spectrum from internal project information to training manuals, but for simplicity the project manager can consider three main categories: internal working documents, product support and maintenance documents and user documents. All types of documentation should be subject to the same rigorous change control procedures although the approval authorities will obviously vary between each type. An index of the documentation of the interrogation system described in Chapter 2 is shown in Fig. 7.1. This can be used as a checklist for similar projects and some further notes are provided at the end of this chapter

7.1 Internal working documents

Some consideration has already been given to this area since it is strongly advised that the project manager establishes standards and procedures for this at the very start of the project. Essentially what is needed is a central technical filing system, mechanisms for publication and recording of technical proposals, together with brief descriptions of reasons for their acceptance or rejection, and a project log to record significant technical decisions, agreements and targets.

To this list can be added the Functional Requirements Specification and the Project Constraints Document which form the

INTERROGATION SYSTEM   ID/IS/17

Index of Documentation

1.   Specification Documents   Ref. No.

         Functional Requirements Specification   FRS/IS/2
         Project Constraints Document   PCD/IS/3
         Functional Specification   FS/IS/5

2.   Design Documents

         Design Strategy   DS0/IS/2
         Design Specification Level 1   DS1/IS/3
         Design Specification Level 2, Vol.1   DS2.1/IS/6
         Design Specification Level 2, Vol.2   DS2.1/IS/5

3.   Implementation Documents

         Flow Charts   I1/IS/0
         Index to Computer Code Files   I2/IS/4
         Catalogue of Implementation Tools   I3/IS/7

4.   Testing Documents

         Test Strategy   QA1/IS/2
         Test Specifications   QA2/IS/6
         Catalogue of Tests and Reference
                             Material   QA3/IS/8

5.   User Documents

         Introduction to the IS   U0/IS/3
         Outline User Specification   U1/IS/3
         Detailed Facility Description   U2/IS/5
         Operating Instructions   U3/IS/3
         Guide to Release Files   U4/IS/2
         Guide to Other Documentation   U5/IS/3

6.   Release Documents

         Release Notices   R1/IS/1-6
         Release Files   R2/IS/4

7.   Miscellaneous

         Project Filing System Index   PF/IS/14
         Project Log   PL/IS/1-4
         Planning Material   PP/IS/1-3

Fig. 7.1. A Documentation Index

objectives for the project as a whole. The FRS also forms a good basis for expansion into a total Function Specification of the product. This should show not only the facilities which are to be provided but an indication of how they are to be implemented and how they interact. It must effectively translate the performance and reliability requirements into terms meaningful to the implementors. This should lead to a set of design specifications for individual components, and the design process will in turn produce a set of coding specifications for modules. This set of documents – Functional Requirements Specification, Functional Specification, Design Specifications and Coding Specifications – should form a hierarchy through which it is possible to trace from any required facility down to its implementation code, or in which one can place a particular module in the context of the system as a whole.

Other internal documentation will automatically build up as the project progresses – design documentation, flow charts, listings, results – and will be used throughout the life of the project. However, since this information will also be vital for maintenance and support purposes, it is worthwhile considering it from the beginning in that context to ensure that what will be produced satisfies both purposes from the outset and a translation process is not required later. One very important way of ensuring that source listings will be of use is to impose from the beginning standards for source comments and layout. Each module should be preceded by a large comment describing its use, method of operation, use of data, etc. – essentially a contraction of the coding specification of Fig. 3.4. In addition the source of text itself should contain comments to aid understanding especially at branch points and labels where flow of control can be difficult to detect merely by reading the code.

Good layout of source can also help readability. Unfortunately, there are other aims which run counter to this. A programmer preparing his own input may well punch the minimum number of characters to save typing and avoid errors, and this does not normally produce clean, reasonable listings. Again well-presented source may contain many spaces and blank lines and, depending on the filing system used, this may occupy more storage space than necessary. An alternative approach is to use a tidying program to produce clean listings after the completion of development. Several such programs are available commercially or through computer users' associations. Similar packages can also be used to produce *post hoc* flow charting although this can never be regarded as a substitute for flow charting or some similar display convention during design.

Plans can also be considered as project documentation although their use is more ephemeral and they are unlikely to be as useful during the maintenance phase as the other documents produced during the project phases. As earlier chapters have stressed, however, they are valuable reference material and should be preserved in a tidy manner.

.2 Product support and maintenance documents

The implementation team should be controlled by the ultimate objectives, specified in the FRS and PCD. The support programmer on the other hand is much more interested in what has actually been implemented rather than what the original intention was. His most important tool is probably the design description but it is essential that this description is of the currently issued product and not of some, as yet unproduced, perfect system.

The hierarchical design description, described in the section on design, is of great help to the support programmer but all too often it is neglected in later stages of the production cycle and restrictions or alterations are defined independently whenever a release is made. Although it is sensible to retain the 'perfect' end design as a consistent document, modifying it only under change control when permanent changes are made, it is also worthwhile to insist that when any intermediate release is made a list of all changes to, or restrictions on, the design description is published for the support programmers. This should refer back to the original document and be as far as possible in the same format. If programmers with support and maintenance experience are available it is a good idea to have them vet the design documentation before coding begins; if it does not satisfy their needs, it is doubtful whether it is satisfactory for use in the project either.

Another important aspect of documentation which is vital to support programmers and which is often forgotten is concerned with implementation tools. These tools will be used by support programmers to maintain and modify the product and the tools themselves may need maintenance. For this reason the tools should be well documented from a user point of view as well as having their own design and implementation documents.

Support programmers will also need flow charts, compiler listings and other computer-produced details of the product. Two points are important here. First, it is essential to make sure that these items correspond to the actual issued versions. This may sound simple but in practice listings are often of items at least one version older than that actually issued and this can cause enormous confusion. Second, it should be possible to refer from individual module listings back to the corresponding coding specification and design details. Both these points can be solved by the rigorous adoption of naming conventions for issues of modules, systems and subsystems and by insistence that all listings, etc., are appropriately titled. The latter is better achieved automatically by making the listing program do it than by relying on manuscript amendments.

Finally, an area of documentation which could be of immense value to support programmers, but which they rarely receive, is the testing documents. Knowing what testing has been done can be of considerable help in locating user reported errors and testing material itself is often very useful as a reference test when modifications have been made.

7.3 User documents

Although implementation and support staff place different emphasis on the documentation they use, their requirements are essentially the same. Users have a completely different set of interests requiring details of what the product will do and how it can be provoked to do it, rather than how it does it. On the other hand it is necessary to keep these two sets of documents linked so that changes in design can automatically be reflected in changes in the user interface, and vice versa. Producing user documentation from the outset is also a useful discipline for keeping programmers' feet on the ground. The most aesthetically pleasing facilities are worthless if the user cannot make use of them.

The best way to start is to expand the FRS again but this time into

100

a User Specification. This is a document which describes facilities in user terms and shows how to invoke them. It should be produced in collaboration with the customer and should be vetted by prospective users. Any feedback should be passed to the designers immediately since the emphasis that the users place on particular aspects may well influence the design. It is particularly important that the User Specification includes as many examples as possible of actual use to which the product is expected to be put. Examples are the easiest way of explaining to a user what he is really being offered but have the added advantage of keeping the implementor in touch with what the user intends to do. A good User Specification is a valuable tool during the implementation of the project and should be known and understood by all project staff.

The final user documentation should also be produced well in advance of the first issue and again should involve close collaboration with the customer and potential users. It is worth trying to persuade one or more users to agree to assist in its production. The first step is to agree with the users the basic objectives: for example, should the documentation be biased towards training new people in the use of the product or as a point of reference for experienced users. Following this it is worthwhile producing a list of contents and perhaps a draft section for discussion with the users. Each subsequent section should be vetted by the users as it appears. If the size of the project or volume of documentation requires it, it may be necessary to employ professional authors. If so, it is important that each member of the team understands that this does not absolve him from actually producing reference material. The author should be regarded basically as an editor and professional rewriter, not as an original source, and technical staff must set aside time to inform him and vet his output.

The final user documentation, like the User Specification, should contain as many examples of use as possible, which must be vetted by the project staff. One important aspect, often neglected, is the operational instructions for the product: what support software or hardware it needs, how it is loaded and so on. The potential operators need as good a service in this respect as other potential users.

It is vital that the user documentation is complete (if not prettily printed) by the time that system validation starts since it is as important to validate the documentation as it is the product. Try to use the product strictly according to the rules of the documentation and see that they agree. If the user documentation was started in good time it should, like the design documentation, describe a 'final' product. If restricted intermediate issues are to be made the project manager should arrange for any restrictions or errors to refer back as far as possible to the user documentation (as well as to the design documentation). Nothing annoys users more than to find by trial and error that the obscure technical jargon in a release notice actually means that a facility they expected does not work.

Finally, remember that the user documentation needs maintenance and support as much as the product itself and the 15 per cent overhead does not necessarily disappear at the end of implementation.

7.4 Examples

Fig. 7.1 is the index of documentation of the Interrogation System, whose early fortunes we followed in Chapters 2 and 3, as it appears some time after issue of the system. The first thing to notice is that even for a relatively simple project the number of documents is considerable. It is actually larger than this list implies since, as we shall see in a moment, several are merely references to material contained elsewhere.

The first two documents, the Functional Requirements Specification and the Project Constraints Document, are the latest issues of the original 'ends and means' documents described in Chapter 2. They are now mainly of historical interest although useful to new maintenance staff wishing to obtain an over-all feel for the project. The Functional Specification is of greater use in this context. This was produced at the beginning of the design stage (see Chapter 3). It expanded each of the functional requirements into implementor understood terms and gave an indication of how they would be provided in the final designs. In this particular project this document was used mainly for training junior designers and as an aid to maintenance and enhancement. The project was simple enough for the Design Strategy document to be produced directly from the FRS and PCD as described in Chapter 3. In even simpler projects

102

the Design Strategy and Functional Specification could be rolled together, while for more complex projects they can be considered as sequential steps between system specification and design.

The Design Strategy document is the one produced by the project manager and his senior design staff and contains an outline design, lists standards to be employed and runs to six or seven pages. The more detailed level 1 document was described in Chapter 3 and its contents list is in Fig. 3.2. Level 2 documents are at the level of coding specifications for individual modules and subsystems and run to two volumes.

Implementation documents are less coherent than the previous sections. The Flow Charts document is merely an indexed file of flow charts and other design/implementation diagrams produced during the detailed implementation. These have been tidied up slightly after the first issue for use as a support and maintenance reference aid and are now kept up to date when modifications or new issues are made by the maintenance team. Similarly, rather than keep reference copies of source listings, which can quickly get out of date, the source for the system is kept on a computer file. Another file contains a catalogue of the modules together with their version numbers. This is essentially an updated version of the interrogation register of Fig. 3.6. A third file lists any modifications made to the issued system below source level. Anyone wishing to see a source listing may request it at a terminal or on a printer and, if the latter, has the chance of using a tidying program to lay it out nicely. The document I2/IS/4 describes these computer files and the methods of accessing them. The Catalogue of Implementation Tools is also a reference document and gives only a brief description of each tool and its use together with details of the individual specification documents for the tool. If, for example, a special language has been produced to implement a project, the document for this language system may be of the same order of magnitude as that for the product itself. The tools documentation can be at least as important to the maintenance of the products as the product documentation itself, particularly the 'user' description of the implementation tools and lists of restrictions and errors.

The Testing Documents were also described in Chapter 3. The Test Strategy, whose contents page is shown in Fig. 3.5, is the original document drawn up by the project manager and his quality controller. This is again mainly of historical interest after issue of the product, but the Test Specification documents for individual modules and subsystems are often of great help in tracking down bugs in the issued system. Of even greater use is the Catalogue of Tests and Reference Material since this provides valuable methods of regression testing when modifications are made. Its format is approximately the same as that of the Catalogue of Implementation Tools and it contains not only the original test and validation methods produced or collected during the project, but is also kept up to date with new tests collected as part of error investigations, etc., which can exercise the system in important ways.

The first of the user documents, the 'Introduction' is a training document for new users which outlines the system and intended user. This is the only training document produced, all other user documentation being essentially reference material from a user point of view. The Outline User Specification is another expansion of the FRS, this time in user terms, while the Detailed Facility Description provides a reference document for the system functions and methods of invoking them. The Operating Instructions are primarily for the computer staff and describe how to set up, load and operate the interrogation system and on what hardware and basic software facilities it relies. The Guide to Release Files shows users how to access and understand the contents of the files documented under section 6. Finally, under user documentation, it is realised that some users may require more detailed insight into the system than others. Rather than provide these users with special documents the Guide to Other Documentation describes the working and maintenance documents and suggests how the interested user can find his way about them.

Each time a new release of the system is made it is accompanied by a Release Notice which describes changes from the previous release and details restrictions and known errors or limitations in terms of modifications to the user documentation. These release notices are all kept although in general only the latest one is of interest. Also associated with a release is a file of errors and reports of suspected errors, together with ways of avoiding them where possible, and hints on features to use and not use in this particular release (as opposed to the system as designed) in order to get the best use out of it. These are held on the computer itself and are updated continuously, not only when a new release is made, but as errors are reported and fixes applied. The system for this has again been developed out of the computerised integration register mentioned in the examples of Chapter 3. The Release Files document lists the files and describes the implementation of the methods of viewing and editing them. The User Guide document, U4/IS/2, tells a user how to access them.

Finally, the miscellaneous section of documentation includes all those items which were vital during the implementation but are now archived. There is an index and guide to the central technical filing system, the Project Log and preserved copies of all plans, slip charts and milestone descriptions. Important conclusions and examples from these documents will have been incorporated in the end of project review report, described in Chapter 5, which is itself kept as an appendix to the project log.

8 Conclusions

Previous chapters have dealt with the project manager's job both relative to the phases of the project and orthogonally with respect to the various aspects of implementation of a software product. Fig. 8.1 pulls together these two viewpoints as a table which a project manager can use as a checklist as he works through the various stages of a project.

Of the column headings in this figure, two are peculiar to the management of a technical development project: technical aspects and documentation. The remainder are merely project management manifestations of the classical management duties of planning, organising and controlling. The only remaining management function not covered is that of leading: motivating, communicating, selecting and developing people. For the project manager this task does not alter in principle from that of any other manager. Differences in detail arise because of the necessity for the project manager's active involvement in day-to-day operating. A manager of a production process, for example, needs to pay only a little attention to the actual mechanics of production since these are in general well defined and he can deal with problems on an exception basis. The project manager, on the other hand, is concerned with a development where the rules for progress are not well known and since he will be constantly called upon to make technical decisions he must be much more aware of detailed implementation matters. The dangers of this involvement with operations, as opposed to classical management (i.e. obtaining results through others) are two. First, it is easy to become obsessed with details instead of concentrating on the over-all progress to the ultimate goal, the release of the product. The techniques and approaches proposed in previous chapters have been designed as far as possible to counteract this tendency but it is worth while for the project manager consciously to step back from the coalface at regular

MANAGEMENT ASPECTS

PROJECT PHASES	P.M.'S MAJOR CONCERNS	ORGANISATION & ADMIN	TECHNICAL	PLANNING	MONITORING	DOCUMENTATION	CHANGE CONTROL
FIRST STEPS	PROJECT DEFINITION	GET A 'CUSTOMER' / DECIDE TEAM ORGANISATION AND RELATIONSHIP OF P.M.	CARRY OUT FEASIBILITY STUDY IF REQUIRED / ESTABLISH FUNCTIONAL REQUIREMENTS	PRODUCE AND AGREE / – OUTLINE PLAN / – STAFF AND FINANCIAL BUDGETS / – RECRUITMENT PLAN	DEFINE STANDARDS FOR MILESTONES	ESTABLISH / – PROJECT LOG / – CENTRAL FILING SYSTEM / PRODUCE: / – FRS – PCD	ESTABLISH CHANGE CONTROL PROCEDURE / CONTROL FRS, PCD
DESIGN — Outline Design			ESTABLISH: / – DESIGN STANDARDS / – DESIGN METHODOLOGY	PRODUCE TESTING AND VALIDATION STRATEGY		ESTABLISH MECHANISM FOR RECORDING THE DESIGN DEFINITION	
DESIGN — Detailed Design	CONTROL OF INTERACTIONS BETWEEN DESIGN AREAS AND BETWEEN STAFF	ENCOURAGE: / – COMMUNICATION / – SEMINARS / – INTERACTION WITH CUSTOMER	CHOOSE IMPLEMENTATION LANGUAGES AND TOOLS / ESTABLISH: / – TESTING STRATEGY / – IMPLEMENTATION STANDARDS / ENSURE MEASURABILITY / ORGANISE: / – WALK THROUGHS / – CROSS CHECKS	PRODUCE AND AGREE: / PERFORMANCE, FACILITY RELIABILITY AND MACHINE TIME BUDGETS / TESTING AND VALIDATION PLAN / LOWER LEVEL PLANS	ESTABLISH: / – MILESTONES / – EXCEPTION ALERT REPORTING / – GRAPHS, SLIP CHARTS REPORTS	PRODUCE: / – DESIGN DOCUMENTATION HIERACHY FOR DATA MODULES AND INTERFACES / – FULL FUNCTIONAL SPECIFICATION / – USER SPEGIFICATION	CONTROL: / – DESIGN / – DEFINITION / – PLANS / – BUDGETS
DESIGN — Design Validation				ESTABLISH COMPATIBILITY BETWEEN LEVELS OF PLAN / DEFINE REPLAN POINTS		DEFINE USER AND SUPPORT REQUIREMENTS	
PROJECT IMPLEMENTATION — Code	CONTROL OF INDIVIDUAL PROGRESS AGAINST PLAN	FORMALLY BEGIN CODING / DEFINE FIXING/ UPDATING MECHANISMS AND STANDARDS	ENFORCE CODING STANDARDS / PRODUCE TEST MATERIAL / RECORD BUG RATE STATISTICS	VALIDATE AND REFINE ASSUMPTIONS AND ESTIMATING TECHNIQUES	OPERATE EXCEPTION ALERT SYSTEM	KEEP FRS, PCD DESIGN DOCUMENTATION IN STEP WITH ACTUAL IMPLEMENTATION	CONTROL: / – PLANS / – DESIGN AND IMPLEMENTATION DOCUMENTATION
PROJECT IMPLEMENTATION — Unit Test					CHECK AGAINST UNIT AND SUBSYSTEM MILESTONES		
PROJECT IMPLEMENTATION — Integrate and System Test	CONTROL OF INTERACTIONS BETWEEN MODULES, SUBSYSTEMS AND DESIGN, IMPLEMENTATION AND TESTING STAFF	ESTABLISH / – ORGANISATION OF TESTING / – ORGANISATION OF INTEGRATION / – DAY TO DAY INVOLVEMENT OF P.M.	OPERATE FIXING/ UPDATING PROCEDURES / TUNE WHEN COMPLETE SYSTEM AVAILABLE	REPLAN AS REQUIRED AND/OR AT REPLAN POINTS	MONITOR ALL BUDGETS / ORGANISE AUDITS AND REVIEWS / CHECK AGAINST SYSTEM MILESTONES AND DEMONSTRA-TIONS	PRODUCE: / USER DOCUMENTATION / SUPPORT DOCUMENTATION	CONTROL: / – PLANS / – DESIGN, IMPLEMENTATION AND USER DOCUMENTATION / – CODE ISSUE SUPPORT / – DOCUMENTATION
PROJECT IMPLEMENTATION — System Validate		ORGANISE: / – VALIDATION TEAM / – FIELD TESTING			END OF PROJECT REVIEW AND REPORT	VALIDATE ALL DOCUMENTATION	
MAINTENANCE & ENHANCEMENT	SERVICE TO USERS	OPERATE USER SUPPORT SYSTEM		ENHANCEMENT PLAN?		MAINTAIN DOCUMENTATION	

Fig. 8.1. Project Manager's Checklist

intervals and consider more strategic issues. Second, it is also easy to overlook the man-management aspects of any management post and to forget that software producers need motivating, counselling, job satisfaction and recognition as much as any other worker. This activity cannot be done at regular intervals, unfortunately, but must be a continuous process. There should probably be another column to Fig. 8.1 which says, for all phases, 'consider staff needs'.

Luckily for the project manager, project organisation has a number of significant compensating advantages in the 'people' area. To begin with, the active involvement of the project manager in all aspects of the development blurs the him/us distinction and eases communication between the manager and his subordinates. Secondly, the fact that a project has a well-defined goal means that it is much simpler for the manager to obtain from his staff a sense of involvement with the project and commitment to it. It is easier for individual staff to think of themselves as part of a team with a leader rather than a work force with a director, and any good project manager can capitalize on this sense of involvement to assist him in motivation and general man-management.

Finally, the project manager himself gains enormously from the dedication to the completion of the product that this form of operation brings. Certainly the satisfaction induced by the successful completion of a software development to previously specified criteria by a dedicated project team is something that is difficult to equal in any other management situation.

References

1. Naur, P. and Randell, B. (eds). Software Engineering: Report on a Conference Sponsored by the NATO Science Committee, Garmisch, Germany, 7th-11th October 1968, *NATO* (January 1969).

2. Buxton, J. N., and Randell, B. (eds). Software Engineering Techniques: Report on a Conference Sponsored by the NATO Science Committee, Rome, Italy, 27th-31st October 1969, *NATO* (April 1970).

3. Richards, M., BCPL, a tool for Compiler Writing and Systems Programming, *Proc. AFIPS*, Vol. 34 (SJCC, 1969).

4. Wirth, N., PL360, a Programming Language for 360 Computers, *JACM*, Vol. 15 no. 1 (1969).

5. Pearson, D., Computer Aided Design and Evaluation System, *Computer Weekly* (26 July, 2 August, 9 August 1973).

6. Heller, R., *The Naked Manager* (Barrie & Jenkins Ltd, 1972).

7. Brooks, F. P., 'Why is the Software Late', *Data Management* (August 1971).

8. Baker, F.T., Chief Programmer Team Management of Production Programming, *IBM Systems Journal*, No. 1 (1972).

9. Urwick Dynamics Ltd (for the Central Computer Agency), *Estimation, Planning and Control of Programming Activities* (H.M.S.O. 1974).

10 *CPLI Language Reference Manual* (Cap-Sogeti Logiciel 1975).

11 Ross, D.T. and Schoman, K.E., Structured Analysis for Requirements Definition, *Proceedings of the Second International Conference in Software Engineering, Oct. 13-15, 1976.*

Index

integration, 46
span of 75
cost, see also *budget, financial*
analysis, 7
change, 8
effectiveness, 36-37, 84, 93
project, 25, 51
CPL1, 31, 109(10)
critical path, 55, 58, 60, 62, 67
analysis, see PERT
cross check, 37, 55-56, 92-93
customer, *8*, 12, 18, 26, 31-32. 38, 41,
43, 48, 52, 54, 63, 77, 91, 101

D

David, E.E., 36, 109(1)
decision record, 10, 75, 91, 95-96
demonstration, 14, 81
dependency, 14, 51, *57*, 84
design, *25-26*
audit, 29
complexity, 30
control, 29, 109(5)
description, 28, 99
documentation, 28, 46, 98-99, 103
language, 27, 109(5), (11)
method, 27
standard, 27, 46
strategy document, 46, 103
validation, 29
desk checking, 37, 93
development, 4
cycle, 25
Dijkstra, E.W., 37, 109(2)
disaster, 8, 12, 31, 76, 84
documentation, 14, 22, 43, 56, *91*, see
also *FRS*, *PCD*
change, 36
'chaser', 36
design, 28, 46, 98, 99, 103
hierarchy, 28, 43, 98, 99
maintaining, 102
maintenance, 43, 98, *99*
operational, 101, 104
reference, 101, 104
support, 98, *99*
test, 100, 103
training, 101, 104
tool, 99, 103-104
user, *100*, 104

validation, 38
duration, see *timescale*

E

editor, 31-32
efficiency, 30, see also *performance*, *cost*
effectiveness
engineering, 5, 109(1), (2)
enhancement, 10, 25, 36, *41*
EPL, 36, 109(1)
error
correction, 35, 42, 63
rate, 40, 42
reporting, 35
statistics, 35
estimating, 54, 95, see also *prediction*
methodology, 55
expenditure curve, see *resource curve*
experience estimating method, 55

F

facilities, *12*, 16, 19, 54, 59, 82, 84, see
also *FRS*
fallback, 84
familiarisation, 49, 58
tool, 32, 77
feasibility study, 9, 18
field test, 39
filing
system, see *project file*
utility, 31-32
financial budget, see *budget*
flow chart, 27, 45, 98, 100
forecast, 11, 29, 85, 88, 95, see also
estimating
FRS, *12*, 15, 19, 20, 22, 26, 28, 39,
40-43, 48, 53, 70, 96, 99, 100, 102,
104
functional
requirements, 11-13
requirements specification, see *FRS*
organisation, 78
specification, *28*, 96, 102
testing, 40

G

Graham, R.M., 5, 109(1)
graph, 25, 33, 51, 58-59, 68, 85, 96